Barnes & Noble Critical Studies

General Editor: Anne Smith

Notes for a New Culture

NOTES
FOR A NEW CULTURE
An Essay on Modernism

Peter Ackroyd

BOOKS
10 East 53d St., New York 10022
(a division of Harper & Row Publishers, Inc.)

Barnes & Noble Books
Harper & Row, Publishers, Inc.
10 East 53rd Street
New York

ISBN 0-06-490008-8

LC 75-35035

First Published in the U.S.A. 1976
© 1976 by Peter Ackroyd

Printed and bound in Great Britain
MCMLXXVI

Contents

Editorial Note

One of the most serious hindrances to the development of a truly creative criticism in this century has been the failure of the critic to learn from the artist. Very few can be seen to have taken to heart that most important dictum of the modern, 'I write: let the reader learn to read'. Yet it is not only the reader whose experience is diminished by the narrowness of the critic; writers too have suffered, because he has failed to play his part in teaching them the potential of their art. This study of modernism is a challenge to critic and artist alike, to come forward into our own time, and to *realize* what we know only in theory now.

A.S.

Introduction

This will be the narration of a secret history: a period of one hundred years, from the last decades of the nineteenth century into our own time, that has yet to be brought to adequate recognition. It is an account of the emergence of LANGUAGE as the content of literature and as the form of knowledge; this anonymous entity is still barely within our consciousness, but its rise has already determined a greater death: the death of Man as he finds himself in humanism and in the idea of subjectivity. What I have attempted to do in this book, on a necessarily restricted scale, is to redefine the context of intellectual tradition and cultural change—and to this end I have used an internal dynamic which can only be assumed. But this is not a scholarly work, it is a polemic and an extended essay directed against our declining national culture. I hope that I have presented the main lines of my argument as clearly as possible, since I decided, from the beginning, to sacrifice any extended analysis of any particular author to this end.

I will distinguish Anglo-Saxon culture from a broadly European one. I will not limit my enquiry to 'poetry', or 'philosophy', or 'literary criticism', since these are separate but not autonomous studies. By invoking a larger spirit it may be possible to re-formulate the ideas of 'culture' and 'tradition' which, in their orthodox forms, have disappeared as silently as ice in a stream. There has been a general transition within European culture which has been either misread or ignored, and I hope to bring this within view, but my central purpose has been to counter the general malaise of English literature and literary studies—by suggesting a spirit and a language of enquiry which will lend them a fresh access of strength.

My thanks must go to the Universities of Cambridge and of Yale, and to the Mellon Foundation, without whose combined help and resources this book might never have been written.

1

The Emergence of Modernism

Le pays de chiméres est en ce monde le seul digne d'être habité.
Il n'y a rien de beau que ce qui n'est pas
La Nouvelle Héloise, Rousseau

The concept of modernism is by no means a recent one. It is, rather, an anachronism which has exerted a powerful force since its inception, and will no doubt continue to do so—the spirit of the 'new' was first invoked in the late seventeenth century, and has yet to be exorcised. That battle of the "Ancients and Moderns", which began in the last decades of the seventeenth century and continued as something of an institution well into the eighteenth, was only the most obvious symptom of a vast transition to which we are the heirs. And if we immerse ourselves in its life, we may come to feel the full force of those definitions we now lightly pass over; if we analyse the ideology of the "Moderns" at the time of its formation, we will recognise what is still the horizon of our own work.

The prevailing temper of the national culture, just after the restoration of the monarchy, was a novel self-consciousness; this mood is now generally taken to be the indispensable context of modernism, but, if so, it is one that has lost its first innocence. For the self-consciousness of the Restoration is a species of wonder: it was a time that set itself apart from all previous ages and cultures, one that looked at itself and marvelled. Sprat's *History of the Royal Society* or Locke's *Essay Concerning Human Understanding* are described as 'representative' texts in the sense that they affirm, and indeed represent, a hiatus in cultural history; their work is conceived as a new beginning, without precedent or

11

historical analogy. In the eighteenth century, this mute anti-historicism becomes a general and systematic scepticism about the nature of history and of 'change', but it is more instructive to recognise the vocabulary and the direction of the first polemics.

Dryden's critical essays and prefaces, for example, contain the first signs of anti-historicism in English criticism, and in Dryden's description of Shakespeare, in *Essay on Dramatic Poesy of the Last Age*, there emerges a theme which seems wholly alien to the matter and manner of modern criticism: "he wanted the benefit of converse . . . the tongue in general is so much more refined since Shakespeare's time". This is the obsession of the age, and there are many texts to sustain it. In his sermons, South derides "the mean, heavy, careless and insipid address" of the preachers of the earlier part of the century. Thomas Sprat argues for the distinction of his time in "that we generally love to have Reason set out in plain, undeceiving expressions". This tone and style of a 'new' writing becomes received truth in a work like John Dunton's *The Post Boy Rob'd of His Mail*, a romance reaching the heart of the new middle-class: "If your sentences were less artfully twin'd they would be more persuasive of the Reality of your Passions."

These examples could be multiplied indefinitely, and between them they affirm a life which now seems very strange. The context of the modern was a style of language. In our time, when language has become that worn coin which is passed from hand to hand, it may well be impossible to understand the effect of a certain language and a certain speech; in the period of seventeenth-century modernism, or what can be called the first modernism, it is *the* essential commitment, a central political and social fact. The religious establishment of Tillotson and South, the masters of the new science, and the political orthodoxy of Locke and the middle-classes can all be located within a radically new language. All of their polemic is directed against "eloquence" and "conceits", that apparently opaque style which can spin disputation and subtlety out of thin air, out of nothing. But what is to be the novel language that will rise in the place of eloquence, and which will for the first time embody a true relation between men and the world? There is a sketch of it in Wilkins's *Essay Toward A Real Character and a Philosophical Language*, in which language be-

12

comes a visible system of universal relations. The new language is to name Reason, a new truth which veils the abyss of language and will transform the natural world. What is continuous, plain, familiar, simple, solid, sensible: this is the family of concepts which initiated the modern movement in England. It is only necessary to consider their antonyms to realise the force of what has been banished by the new dispensation of language.

And so the study of modernism can begin at this point. Its new life can go under the name of 'empiricism' or 'natural science', or it can be seen in a larger context which will bring forward what has previously been hidden. In Sprat's *History of the Royal Society* there is a trace of what is to become the most profound revolution which modernism introduced. He is writing about the fatality of eloquence: ". . . the only Remedy, that can be found for this Extravagance: and that has been, a constant Resolution, to reject all the amplifications, disgressions, and swellings of style: to return back to the primitive purity, and shortness, when men delivered so many *things* almost in an equal number of *words*".

Words, then, are to be stamped in the image of things; they are to be plain and they are to be transparent. They are to reflect 'things'. Language comes to be of secondary value, significant only in terms of its reportorial status. An extension of this appears in Locke's account of language, in which it is considered to be the result of an artificial contract; words are man-made and derive from natural objects, the new solid and simple entities of the modern world. It is from this seemingly slight and obscure origin, culled from texts that are no longer read, that the idea of autonomous 'meaning' first emerges. For it is a world of things and of simple ideas which now stamps its image upon the word, the word which is itself meaning-less except as a transparent token. But to assume that language is a material entity which exists by reason of an original contract is to assume man's control over it. It becomes subordinate to the truths of our social being; this is the ground on which we still walk, since it was this access of meaning which first awakened the modern world.

The banishment of language as autonomous and as an object of knowledge makes way for the primacy of Man. The truth of the Reason that it has been constrained to name instead of itself is primarily a social one, since it is founded upon a notion of shared responses and of a community of judgement. So emerges the "common sense" which will unite authoritative opinion: Thomas Rymer, the dramatic critic, cites "authority for common sense" in his *Tragedies of the Last Age*. A similarly socialised and representative judgement appears in the essays of Sir William Temple: "I have chosen the subject of these essays wherein I taken human life to be most concerned and which are of most common use and necessary knowledge." And just as values return to a mute inglorious presence in the world, so do values leave language and accrue to Man. "Experience" emerges as a concept of value— "While I was thus hammering out some new design on the anvil of experience" (from Richard Head's *The English Rogue*)—and it was to become a concept with an extremely long life. From the beginning there are general truths of 'experience' to be elicited, and the figure who has been shaped by them becomes representative. *The Adventures of the Counterfeit Lady* become, in fact, an extension of the new common sense: " 'Yes indeed,' replied the prisoner, 'I am very like a looking glass wherein you may all see your own frailties'." Language must be effective upon a human scale, and it must become perfectly congruent with the new 'human nature'. The idea of Man is placed at the centre of knowledge, as the repository of all values. It is his activity which becomes the touchstone of the world, and it is within his significance that our culture still dwells.

This was the first access of a self-conscious 'modernism' within English culture, and at a distance of almost three centuries it can be called, paradoxically, the classical modernism. But, even at this late date, it has not yet been recognised for what it was and so it has persisted into our own time without examination. We have never again attained that same level of self-consciousness which was responsible for the original change of direction; and, predictably, it was to be first in France that the new order of classical modernism was understood, and then overturned.

The rational context which sustained classical modernism in England comes to sharpest focus in the typically cerebral and highly organised classicism of the Parisian literary establishment. It is, for example, in Boileau's *Art Poétique* that the new order

14

is given its definitive form; for him, too, the critical appeal must always be outward to an idea of socialised Man, and Boileau is the "honnête homme" who evokes through his own experience a common sense of public and accessible truth which the poem and the poet must embody:

> Aimez donc la raison; que toujours vos écrits
> Empruntent d'elle seule et leur lustre et leur prix

and it is this notion of "la raison" which is most compelling, because most clearly formulated, in France. In French literature of the seventeenth and eighteenth centuries it extended itself over discourse like an opaque fabric, so that all things were known and held in its terms. The constant foci of classical physics and the authoritarian syntax of Racinian drama both bear witness to the steady pressure toward immutability and constancy in a universe of 'meaning'. Its constant presence is at the same time elating and disturbing, it accounts for a world with the values of man but there is no alternative to its highly specific and schematised psychology —a psychology at least in the sense that it concerns itself with the values which man discovers within himself as the source of reason and experience. It is this triad of qualities—unity, harmony and fitness—which share their origin in the idea of *homo cogitans* as absolute presence. So it is that subjectivity can emerge as pure-presence-to-itself. The movement of reason is one that confirms itself in the pure act of thought, an act that resides solely in the mind of man. It is in this context that language is further devalued. For language, pre-eminently in its written state, is non-presence-to-itself. It becomes a secondary presence as a medium for man's speech, and as the trace of speech it is relegated beneath the movement of pure subjectivity.

One of the earliest texts to clarify the relationship between classical modernism and the movement of rationalism is Arnauld's *La Logique ou L'Art de Penser*, published in 1662. His *L'Art de Parler* had described the possibility of a universal grammar, and the central argument had been that language, as an invention or product of the mind, must necessarily bear the imprint of rationality. *L'Art de Penser* defines this rationality. There is a characteristic emphasis that "words are sounds used to express ideas",

15

where ideas are conceived as distinct and positive forces. It is only the ambiguities of language that obfuscate ideas, and these ambiguities can be resolved in true definition and division.

There is nothing remarkable in all of this. The central points are made in three axioms (section IV, 7):

1. All that is contained in the clear and distinct idea of a thing can be truly affirmed of the idea of that thing.

2. Existence, at least possible existence, is included in the idea of whatever we conceive clearly and distinctly.

3. Nothingness cannot be the cause of anything.

These propositions are apparently self-evident, and they are meant to be so. But what is this self-evident status of "Nothingness"? It is no-thing but manages to be the subject of the third axiom and it is through this paradox that our theme develops. In L'Art de Penser nothingness is conceived formally, as a contradiction in the idea of a thing. And similarly, "a negative sentence denies the joining of two ideas". Nothingness is not an entity, and it cannot adhere within language; it is simply the misuse of syntactical relations or sheer obscurantism. The concern is for what is evident, distinct and already known. So it is in Descartes' notion of a *positive* infinite, or an infinite infinite. Malebranche affirms that nothingness "has no properties" and "is not visible". And although Leibniz may make his famous enquiry why there is "something rather than nothing", the matter is conveniently left to one side. Throughout the texts of the time there is the constant presence of this non-existent but troubling 'non-entity'. The literature which locates itself in the space of classical modernism can support its 'meaning' and its common sense only by constructing what is clearly a most precarious positivism. And it is through this hiatus in the surface of French rationalism that new forms of language will eventually emerge.

The writing which does emerge in opposition to classical modernism finds its own space in a recognition of the power of "Nothingness"; it is fed by absence, by what is not admitted and cannot possibly exist in the classical universe. Pascal's sense of

16

infinite space, Bouhours' concept of the necessity of falsehood in creation, Rochester's *Ode to Nothing* suggest the possibility of another language. In England, the pressures against orthodox modernism appear in the 1730's and the 1740's with a poetry of the 'sentimental' and the 'sublime'—there is an appeal to the more ill-defined areas of classical modernism, but it remains within an orthodox rhetoric of human truths albeit in an epic guise. It is only in France, where the authoritarian language of "la raison" receives its sharpest formulations that it can undergo its most profound revaluation. I am not referring here to what are conventionally known as the "Romantics", Hugo and Rousseau and the rest, since they still dwell within a subjectivity that rests upon a philosophy of absolute presence in which language is a secondary, mimetic force. In a sense, the Romantics are the last rationalists. The significant revaluation first appears in the writings of the Marquis De Sade. It is in his work that we discover the voice of what will become the 'modernism' of our own time, since his work is as self-conscious and as anti-historical as that of the first 'moderns'.

De Sade discovers what classical discourse unsays; it is what has been already called, with the hopeless insufficiency of its connotations, nothing. This may seem paradoxical, faced with De Sade's use of the technical surfaces of classical discourse; his concern for a precise numerology, his use of rhetorical *exempla* and argument and his minute analysis of individual passion—"There is more to it than just experiencing sensation, they must also be analysed", as one heroine puts it at a provoking moment—place him well within the forms of the seventeenth- and eighteenth-century *novella*. De Sade embodies perverse sexuality into crypto-arithmetical forms, but this is part of a gigantic parody reminiscent of the attempts to found a universal grammar on the assumption that language is 'rational'. De Sade seizes upon and systematises what is, precisely, irrational. Man's passions are necessarily irritants to the conceiving mind, but in De Sade they are given the positive status which was once given only to distinct ideas. Nature is a malevolent and destructive force; belief in the socialised truths of Man is a crime and the supreme belief, in the absolute presence of God, is the supreme crime. Even specific acts of evil

17

smear, by making local and visible, the transcendental Nothing, that complete annihilation of 'values', of which De Sade's figures are the saints. The master, in De Sade's notion of the master/slave relationship, embodies his own values far beyond the landscape of human truths: "Oui, nous sommes les dieux," says the Abbess Delbène in *Juliette*.

This reification of Nothing, embodied in paradox and contradiction and admitted for the first time within an ostensibly classical form, evokes a life which orthodox modernism could not recognise. De Sade denies those values upon which its particular social ethic, of meaning and of human value, is based. The Abbess Delbène says, "The total disappearance of Mankind would grieve Nature very little". But what can exist without Man? His values, and the meaning of his values, have their centre everywhere and their circumference nowhere. The body of classical discourse is expressly designed to promote what must be so. And it is now in the work of De Sade that we can see for the first time the shadow which this ostensibly transparent discourse has thrown unawares.

De Sade has of course been made the parent of a French genealogy; the writings of Lautreamont, Rimbaud and Baudelaire have been seen to constitute a vision of revolt and self-annihilation that can be first traced in De Sade's own work. But this is simply on the thematic surface and theirs is a revolution of content only, since they retain a classical presence in their own work which is mediated through an inherited and positive speech. The central transition is in fact one that divides De Sade as much from Baudelaire as it does from Boileau: it is the emergence of the idea of 'literature'. It is this idea which separates classical modernism from the modernism of our own time, and it propels us into our time with a name so familiar that it seems to have no origin. But it does have an origin—and it also has a history. It first comes into the light, as a conceived entity, in the writing of Gustave Flaubert, He is the first modern writer to detach his 'presence' from his own writings, so that the language sustains itself with its own weight. An unbroken object appears, without a first or second person singular to lead us back to ourselves with commentary or admonishment.

There is a sentence in one of Flaubert's letters which makes

18

the point for me: "What seems beautiful to me and what I should like to do is a book about nothing, a book with no exterior attachment." There is a similar sentence in Racine's preface to *Bérénice*: "All invention consists in making something out of nothing," but it does not have the same sense. For Racine, "nothing" is not an absence or a lacuna but simply a space to be filled: his especial 'literature' is invention, or a division of that rhetoric which uses language as an instrument of meaning. It is in Flaubert's other 'literature' that the language breaks itself off from this man-made entity; it appears in his novels as "about nothing", it does not represent or correspond to the realm of solid objects and simple truths which is Man's primary domain. Literature is a subject without an object. And Flaubert's remark that "the only truth in this world is a well-made sentence" proposes a new kind of value, more precarious than any before. For if language takes over its own space for the first time then the 'nothing' which it celebrates, that silence which surrounds its proper authority, will also appear for the first time. Can it be chance, for example, that the concepts of guilt and anxiety appear in the work of Kierkegaard after the deconstruction of systematic philosophy?

What is, in fact, the 'anxiety' of Rimbaud and Baudelaire in the work that follows Flaubert? What they place in most doubt is not 'life' or 'values' (although that has often been claimed for them) but rather the status of the poetic activity itself. And it is their will to 'live out' their poetry which gives a fresh access of anxiety because of their recognition, like that of Flaubert, that it is indeed "about nothing". The purity and abstractness of Baudelaire's line, for example, generate a symbolism of "le Néant", "le vide" and "le nu". The revolutionary idea of literature becomes for him a dilemma of experience (a word whose origin can be recalled from earlier texts) to be personalised and transformed into an interior drama. It is not mediated within the work itself. Baudelaire's concept of the dandy, aloof from the crowd and seeking the night, in his life metaphor for the peculiar status of literature. And it is only Mallarmé who mediates the presence of "le Néant" within the poem itself, and thus masters the space which Flaubert had opened between his words and the world.

Mallarmé is, in a sense that has now turned a full circle, the first of our 'moderns'; his sustained interrogation of his language and his admission of its own self-consciousness make apparent what had before been confused and submerged. He says in *Quant Au Livre*: "Everything exists to end in a Book", which is his literature. The world of discrete objects is gathered up into a single subject, the Book, which is the material presence of the Word and which claims no object. Another sentence from the same essay of Mallarmé's emphasises his connection with the writings of Flaubert: "L'emploi elementaire du discours dessert l'universal reportage dont, *la littérature exceptée*, participe tout entre les genres d'écrits contemporains."

If this new literature, then, is not reportorial and not mimetic, and if it embodies no other value than its own, it must for Mallarmé come to claim an absolute status. Even the author has to disappear from the text in order to allow the words to emerge fully into their own being. The rationalist-romantic 'I', which continued and still continues to exert so powerful a spell within our own culture, now disappears almost without trace. And if it does emerge in the poem, it is only to be condemned to a sterile contemplation of its own image, as insubstantial as the names it forces to contain it—this is the Narcissus of late symbolist poetry.

But how can we read these words that appear to have no origin? They claim an inverted presence on the page, a hollowness full of echoes, by describing the absence of the object:

> Mais, chez qui du rêve se dore
> Tristement dort une mandore
> Au creux néant musicien

The rhythmic and harmonic tightness of the poetry serves to strengthen the absence of denotative meaning, and we cannot look to the line to form a unified response to the whole poem since each word has a distinctive texture, a depth of connotation, which is only formally carried over into the whole. The harmonic associations of "dore", "dort" and "mandore" enrich the interior of the poem while counterpointing the flatness and silence of denotative meaning which surrounds it. While the ostensible content of the poem is "nothing" ("the musician of hollow nothingness" and so

20

on) the syllables have a responsiveness and variation which stay on their own ground.

We cannot, of course, misread the traces of human consciousness and human organisation out of the existence of the poem; the resonance of Mallarmé's language comes in large part from a recognition that it is not, and can never be a natural object. Discourse cannot achieve an absolute identity with itself; here are the opening words of a poem that make use of this fact:

> Mes bouquins refermés sur le nom de Paphos

which is, *my* antique books have been closed again. This "my" exists in an equivocal relation to its books and their images. They are "closed", but what about the Book which is the form of Mallarmé's endeavour? The poem continues:

> Coure le froid avec ses silences de faux
> Je n'y hululerai pas de vide nénie
> Si ce très blanc ébat au ras du sol dénie
> A toute site l'homme du paysage faux
>
> Ma faim qui d'aucuns fruits ici ne se régale
> Trouve en leur docte manque une saveur égale. . . .

The length and resonance of the line here suggest a certain relaxation of emphasis as the poem brushes against a sphere of meaning. But this is part of the general ambiguity which unites the poem in the dual capacity of language to both evoke a world of objects and in the same gesture to deny or delete it: the closing couplet here exposes what is running through the rhythmic subtlety and paradoxical fullness ("vide nénie") of the vowels, that the "learned absence", the images of silence and negation, can only be celebrated by a language with rich connotative resources. "Froid", "silence", "blanc", "vide", "manque" are Mallarmé's family of concepts, but they express a positive force.

Language thus establishes the impermanence of being, as it is generally described, since being can be called forth and denied within one and the same act. But by fully evoking this impermanence of being, the poem also calls into question its own permanence. We have seen that, for Mallarmé, the written language does not have the self-assurance or the universality of, for example, the Hegelian λόγος; it is run through with the furrow of differentiation. What, then, can it be 'in itself'?

This new literature may simply be the lacuna between word and object. The themes of Mallarmé's writing are those of distance and separation, and in the following stanza something is evoked which can only become more distant as words are pressed into the service of describing it, until it eventually stands for a general absence:

> Quel sépucral naufrage (tu
> Le sais, écume, mais y baves)
> Suprême une entre les épaves
> Abolit le mât dévêtu

The words here are simply emblems for the memory of things. They have a hardness, a rhythmic fixity, which for the first time seems to restrict their free development. It is as if the absence of a guiding object has left the language without movement of any kind, and the names have become hard shells in which can be heard the false sound of a sea. But what has happened in this process to those other words which once fixed the classical universe: words such as "nature", "reason" and "Man" which connected to a vital presence with a glow of denotation? And who will listen if only language speaks? The Mallarmian analysis offers some sort of answer here, since the name of 'Man' may merely be one more written sign, the trace of a desire which has failed:

> Le néant a cet Homme aboli de jadis,
> "Souvenirs d'horizons, qu'est-ce, o toi, que la Terre?"

These lines reveal the contours of what has become 'the modern'. The troubled epiphany of language in the idea of literature constitutes the end of Man as an epistemological entity. Language has excised the selfhood and the rhetorical world of signs which emerged in the late seventeenth century as the ground of the first modernism. And now on this new ground Nietzsche comes forward.

For Mallarmé, the Book—"architectural et prémédité"—will eventually exist as an unknown explanation of the earth, even if the act of explanation constitutes the 'disappearance' of the earth.

22

But for Nietzsche, the emergence of language into an autonomous life will actually reveal no new truths or new values, but instead it will cast into doubt the very idea of truth. Now that language has recovered its opaqueness and its complexity, it will reveal aspects which have not been recognised before: at this point, we are dealing with Nietzsche the philologist. The notion of the 'text' and its exegesis runs through his work, not simply as a convenient analogy but as the living centre of his design. The world we know and recognise is simply a product of interpretation; values and truths overlay each other in an endless process of exegesis: "There are no things in themselves, and there is no absolute knowledge; the perspectivist, illusory character belongs to existence." The emergence of a written language which excises human meaning has closed the old spaces of certain knowledge, and now refuses certain knowledge even within itself.

Nietzsche actually celebrates this permanent disavowal of meaning. For Flaubert and for Mallarmé, it had been a "nothingness" which had both beckoned and astonished them. But for Nietzsche it is an affirmative life, since the denial of meaning opens out into a new world of multiplicity and difference—that dance which unwinds the old unities. "The world has become endless, we cannot dismiss the possibility that it contains endless interpretations." There is no 'being' to be excavated and no absolute truth to which 'we' should aspire; there is only the visible world of process and change: "The senses do not lie. What we *make* of their testimony, that alone introduces lies; the lie of unity, the lie of thinghood, of substance, of permanence. 'Reason' is the cause of our falsification of the senses . . . the apparent world is the only true one." This is Nietzsche's radical departure from the idealistic tradition and his indirect, maieutic method punctures at different angles the absolutes of, for example, Hegelian systematising: "The will to system is a lark of integrity." He invades with his ironies the notion of absolute presence, and of those ultimate 'meanings' and ends which rest upon it. He also stands firmly against that general positivism which was invading certain intellectual circles in France, and which was to develop into the idea of the "science of Man". For Nietzsche, any original text—whether we wish to call it Man or Reason—has long since been overlaid by interpre-

23

tation. If we are to clear the ground a little, the assertion of paradox and contradiction becomes the most relevant philosophical
and poetic activity.

But this continual process of interpretation does not simply
return to the void of unthought. It is Nietzsche's central purpose
to set up an exegesis of the exegetical process itself, and in his
concept of the "will to power" interpretation can become aware
of itself as the enactment of that will: "The truth is that interpretation is a means of gaining mastery over something." The
spirit of life and power exists in a process which has no 'end' other
than to appropriate more of itself, to interpret anew and to gain a
fresh access of power: "to live one must evaluate". Life increases
itself in an ever quickening journey from its origin, the 'text',
which we can no longer identify.

But who are "we"? The process of interpretation can no longer
admit any object but itself—since the text is unknown—but who
is its subject? It is not "Reason" since Nietzsche has already rejected that. Can it be "Man"? But for Nietzsche that sign has
already lost its power: "Man is not the measure of all things . . .
what do 'we' matter?" And since it is our syntax that forms our
judgements for us, perhaps syntax will survive us: "I am afraid
we are not rid of God, because we still have faith in grammar."
So whose voice is it, then, who is doing the interpreting? The
quest of the will to power becomes more difficult at this point.
It is no accident that Nietzsche should ask of the Sphinx, no one's
idea of a fast talker, "Just who is it anyway who has been asking
these questions?"

It is not "I". There is no selfhood or subjectivity to discover
itself within a world of objects and truths: "A thought comes
when it will, not when 'I' will . . . 'I' is only a synthesis created by
thinking". Again and again Nietzsche ridicules the idea of subjectivity, in much the same spirit as Mallarmé had effaced any
authorial warrant from the words which are no longer his. And
Nietzsche does not dwell in the personal world of Baudelaire, where
the 'I' is sick and trembling for departure. Nietzsche's world is one
of health, where it is a strength and not a weakness that the 'selfhood' has departed and that there are multiple forms of interpretation in its place. The spirit of his new philosophy lies in

24

constant evaluation and change, not in the search for a permanent truth of being.

Without this permanent truth to convey, Nietzsche's writing can be dramatic and various; language has become an entity that contains man who wavers between its structures, looking through one gap and then through another. Nietzsche employs the vocabulary of Aristophanes, or the periods of Cicero, or the aphoristic methods of La Rochefoucauld to establish the manifold plasticity of language. These different forms of interpretation illuminate the contours and the particular restrictions of each other, and in so doing they deconstruct the idea of a unified selfhood that speaks through them. Zarathustra "spake" . . . "all existence is a kind of speech" . . . and we live in a universe of sounds that never cease to flow, not in one of single judgement and a conceiving "I".

So if interpretation speaks through us, who is "Man"? As organic existence, he is seen by Nietzsche as a specialisation of the fundamental will to power and thus as a content destined to disappear before its form. Man is a "small, overstrained kind of animal whose days are numbered". It is only the flow of becoming that has permanent form, since it is preserved in Nietzsche's notion of eternal recurrence. But Man "appears as a sickness with which existence is infected . . . I am tired of Man."

This is a long way from any theological or rational humanism. And what has been emerging as an historical analogy during this analysis is the presence of a language that existed before humanism in its orthodox forms. For the universe of classical and medieval discourse has no notion of Man as the source of its values. It spread itself over the Word and its levels of interpretation. Both cultures were capable of playing quite formalistically with different levels of language and thus different types of meaning. In the Athenian dramatic contests, for example, the satyr play quite naturally follows the tragic trilogy; in medieval texts, the 'truth' resides on levels of literal, allegorical, moral and analogical discourse—just as *fabliaux* and religious poetry can be placed side by side to comment upon one another. Theirs is a language very different from that socialised and transparent medium through which facts and values can shine through, and very much more like that in which Mallarmé and Nietzsche have been seen here to work.

25

But if there is a context in Nietzsche that accommodates these multiple levels of discourse, it cannot be their societal or theological one. It is not located in any affirmative principle, as the languages of medieval and classical culture had been, but rather in the fissure between these levels; if there were to be a text, it would reside in the idea of difference itself. The spirit of life exists in the space that holds various truths apart and "we must admit untruth as a necessary condition of life." "Untruth" here comes very close to the idea of "le Néant" and this affirmation of difference and incongruity is at the centre of Nietzsche's argument; the obvious gap between one value and another fires that continual urge to interpret again and again, and to gain the mastery. If the "over-man" comes to destroy the universe of old truths, he will do so by celebrating the principle of un-truth, or no-thing.

Mallarmé and Nietzsche rediscover the power of written language in their return to rhetorical and symbolic forms, thus shifting the ground of knowledge away from Man and the human sciences which try to locate a permanent truth outside language. It is the social scientists who have externalised human needs and thus deprived them of their inner necessity; Mallarmé and Nietzsche do not believe in "I" or "Man" and do not continue them in their troubled existence. Their world becomes one that is engaged in its own process of unfolding, and one in which Man is only a symptom and not a cause. These are the lines of the argument, at least as far as they can be traced in Europe at the beginning of this century. The fact that they are only now being recognised suggests what their promise had been, perhaps, rather than anticipates their fulfilment.

26

2

The Uses of Aesthetics

Much has been learnt.
Many of the heavenly ones has he named,
Since we have been a conversation
And have heard from one another.

                                   Hölderlin

The overturning of the forms of classical modernism is part of an essentially European movement, then, with its foundations in Germany and France. During the same period in England all that can be traced is the survival of that first modernism, rooted in a stubborn philosophical empiricism which becomes so familiar that it loses its form and remains a loose content to be used under any name. Where Mallarmé saw his work as the first self-questioning of language, and Nietzsche drew himself at the head of a tradition of European philosophy, the creative activity of England was filtered through a vague pragmatism of social value. The age itself cultivated this image. Bosanquet, in his pioneering *History of Aesthetics* published in 1892, narrates the formal progress of European aesthetics only to recognise its loss of contact with the Anglo-Saxon world, and then proceeds to cite the work of Ruskin and Morris as the distinctive English contribution in the tradition of Kant, Hegel and Schelling. And this is characteristic. There has been a systematic ignorance or misreading of the European movement in England, with consequences which have only recently become evident.

The writings of Carlyle and Bradley could be adduced here, but the critical texts of Samuel Taylor Coleridge are more than simply representative. He stands between Europe and England as a mediator and reconciler, and his is the major example of an affirmative response to contemporary European poetry and philosophy. The connection of that response with the indigenous spirit of his work will throw a great deal of light on the national culture from which it proceeds. Coleridge's reading and translation of certain of the texts of the German idealistic philosophers, for example, can be seen as an appeal against those empirical procedures which pervaded the national culture and which were even then in the prison of Hume's ultimate scepticism. But the enthusiasm of Coleridge for European philosophy is not simply a reaction against his own. Stuart Mill writes of his formative but *traditional* role: "He had been the great awakener in this country of the spirit of philosophy, within the bounds of traditional opinions." The philosophy may be alien but it is transformed, and it is within those traditional "bounds" that the work of Coleridge actually rests; and it bears witness to a formative presence within English culture.

Coleridge's distinctive contribution to both philosophy and poetics is generally taken to be his affirmation of the selfhood as a moral agent, and of the "Imagination" as the mediator between man and the world. This is very different from Kant's enquiry into the unity of the self in perception, which had been the source of Coleridge's analysis, and the difference—as we will come to see —is characteristically one of moral context. There is a passage in Coleridge's *On Poesy Or Art* which enlarges upon this theme. He is describing the process of artistic creation: "so as to place these images [of nature], totalised and filled to the limits of the human mind, as to elicit from the forms themselves the moral reflexions to which they approximate, to make the external internal, and the internal external, to make nature thought, and thought nature." Mind and nature, man and object are posited in a vital relationship in which both share, and are both transformed by, the same principle of life. This is the principle of mind since "the forms of nature recall, express and modify the thoughts and feelings of the mind". The position of Coleridge here is a humanistic one, and the humanism evoked is one that has as its context an unacknowledged rationalism: the qualities which Coleridge invokes are those of "system", of permanence and unity; and we are to discover their rationale in the mythic union of man and nature. *On Poesy Or*

Art clarifies this union: ". . . in Nature, the thought and the product are one." The yearning toward discovering our form within
the natural world seems also to be a yearning toward that simul-
taneity of natural creation which Coleridge analyses: reason is to
be given the permanence of nature in the same bond which grants
nature the purpose and meaning of reason. The central purpose of
Coleridge's thought, and one which will later be recognised elsewhere, is to retrieve the old unity of man by founding it on enduring and visible principles. This is the 'message' of his humanism.
Art is to be the mediatress of thought and things; its imaginative
unity redeems man from chance and change on the same terms as
it transforms nature into an embodiment of rational law. "Art", as
Coleridge puts it, "humanises Nature."

This goes a long way beyond, or behind, Kant's philosophical
texts although they are still Coleridge's ostensible source. His
concept of "Reason" as the faculty which intuits general principles
is taken over from Kant's dichotomy of Reason and Understanding,
but Coleridge places it within a much older tradition of moral
thought: "Reason is the fountain of all morality." And the central
commitment which takes Coleridge through idealism is primarily
an orthodox moral and teleological one: "Religion is the ultimate
aim of philosophy." Unlike Kant, Coleridge stops short before any
consistent or thorough interrogation of eighteenth-century empiricism; despite his overturning of its content, he affirms on other
terms the socialised and fideistic context which it had first established. A generalised idea of "Man" is placed at the centre of the
world: "Therefore the material world must have been made for
the sake of man, at once the high priest and representative of the
Creator, as far as he partakes of that reason in which the essence
of all things co-exist." The neo-platonic colour here serves to confirm the pervasive orthodoxy of Coleridge's writing, a writing
which stays "within the bounds of traditional opinions"—which
are, in fact, the bounds of humanism and of that extension of
humanism in subjectivity. The criticism of Coleridge is, indeed,
eclectic and disorganised. He does not seem to be aware of the
radical content of his European sources, but simply employs their
terminology as rhetorical constructs in a larger and more traditional perspective. He accommodates a wealth of argument and

descriptive detail without making any consistent attempt to recognise its theoretical context or to revalue its implied aesthetic and social criteria. It is in this sense that his criticism is typically Anglo-Saxon.

The English contemporaries of Mallarmé and Nietzsche do indeed recognise themselves in this light, and if there is one English critic who informs the period with that spirit, it is Matthew Arnold. In his use of a public voice as a vehicle for a public conscience, he is much like Coleridge; in his enthusiasm for European culture, and in his belief in its superiority, his work has a purpose and a significance that emphasise its continuity with that of Coleridge. But it is not in fact to Coleridge, but to the French critic Sainte-Beuve, that Arnold turns as his model. Arnold refers to him as "the most notable critic of our time". And what precisely are those European values which appeal to the English critic?

Sainte-Beuve states in a description of the periodical *Revue des Deux Mondes* that it helped "maintenir publiquement certaines traditions d'art, de goût, et d'études", where the emphasis is upon the significance of a humane culture which is close to Arnold's quest "to know the best that has been thought and said in the world". There is a strain of humanism in the criticism of both, which for Sainte-Beuve is founded not only upon a tradition of values but upon the truth of the individual moral life: ". . . de la véritable, de l'intérieure, de celle qui est morale et humaine." It is of some interest that this appeal to a form of subjectivity, at the very time it was being questioned in the work of Mallarmé and Nietzsche, should appeal to Matthew Arnold in his defence of traditional values. And it is worth noting here that Sainte-Beuve, in his *Causeries du Lundi*, employs an analytic and naturalistic method of criticism which anticipates the approaching "human sciences", or the new humanism.

But the humanism which Arnold shares with Sainte-Beuve is one that is, ostensibly, founded upon a reading of the classical texts; there are many references to, for example, Sophocles and Thucydides. Although Arnold shares the same assumptions as Coleridge he is not a 'Romantic'—Arnold's criticism has as its context a sense of classical texts as somehow 'objective' and unified. This is developed, for example, in his *Preface To Homer*, where the virtues he ascribes to the Homeric epics are those of "a plainness and naturalness of thought . . . simplicity and directness . . . he deals with the object simply and freely." There is to be an absolute affinity of mind and speech, mind and object. It was this affinity, of course, that Coleridge affirmed in the act of "Imagination" and Arnold's canon of values is conceived in this spirit: simplicity, nobleness, directness, plainness. These constitute their common humanism, an affective range in which man is eternally linked to his actions and to the world. For Arnold, as it was for Coleridge, it is not a question of 'style' but of a central moral competence: "The poets of a nation which has produced such a conceit as that [a fanciful simile of Chapman's] must purify themselves in the fire before they can hope to render Homer. They must expel their nature with a fork and keep crying to one another night and day." The edge of mock solemnity here actually confirms the poignancy of Arnold's sense of the decay of humanism and its traditional virtues—the concern for 'antiquity' is, in fact, an awareness of transience and present decay.

But perhaps this sense goes unrecognised under the surface of Arnold's humanism, since at the level of apparent content there is a continuity with those values which emerged in the first age of modernism, in the late seventeenth century. What does it mean for Arnold to be a "poor humanist"? It means to "humanise knowledge"; it is "the study of perfection—true human perfection as a harmonious and general perfection of society." It is a humanism which, naturally, reifies 'man' and establishes itself on a notion of social authority. Ideas of "perfection" and "harmony" are derived from a version of rationalism which subordinates art and language to the criteria of "unity" and "end". The 'meaning' which man finds within himself becomes universal, and "truth and seriousness" become for Arnold indicative of great poetry for poetry is "criticism of life". This is the sense of life which seventeenth-century modernism first discovered, dependent as it is upon the values of socialised man; it is also the same life which Coleridge enforces in his criticism. This is the continuity, the "bounds" of the English critical tradition as it is carried over into our own century. A moral and humanitarian context is imposed upon us, since for

31

Arnold and Coleridge the purpose of culture is "to make reason and the will of God prevail".

But it is never enough to rest at the level of content, when the central fact which confronts the reader is that of Arnold's language. It seems transparent even when it has been most carefully arranged, and its formal devices generate what is taken to be the autonomous 'meaning' of the prose. It employs that "neutral" style which is elaborated by seventeenth-century modernism, and which determines Arnold's public role. His assumption of a *persona* in *Culture and Anarchy* is indicative of this: "as clearness is the one merit which a plain, unsystematic writer, without philosophy, can hope to have . . . without generalities . . . close to the level ground of common fact." This is close to the voice of Locke: "I must appeal to experience and observation whether I am in the right . . . I pretend not to teach but to enquire," and to the whole tone of the first moderns. Arnold's prose is relaxed and accessible, affirming certain 'truths' and appealing to the standards and the common sense of a humane 'public' which, as always, is a rhetorical construct. Since the writings of Arnold are now being read as representative of his period, it should be noted that his is essentially a backward look. His is a fine missionary humanism but it is one that carries its own decay within itself. Arnold adopts a moral and theoretical context, the origins of which remain undisclosed. He is no more able than Coleridge to confront the pervasive traditionalism of our national culture, which runs below the particular issues which he addresses himself to. It is, in fact, only now that the ground can be cleared a little.

So the humanism which Arnold and Coleridge share is one that lies in a belief in the primacy of man as a social concept and, more importantly, within his individual moral being. And if there is a characteristic 'romanticism' within the culture, it is the reification of this selfhood into a moral agent which finds its own reflection in a natural order. Kant's earlier postulate of the unity of natural consciousness in "apperception" lends a certain theoretical élan to this native idea, but this is employed only as a formula within an older and more orthodox context. This orthodoxy does not of course recognise itself as such, and it still remains a tenuous force even when it has been cast into most doubt.

The 'I' of moral experience, for example, remains a substantial presence in the poetry of the 'first romantics' but it starts its gradual process of decay in the writings of the Victorian poets. Although it stays at the centre of their design, it needs to be sustained by a formal harmony of rhyme and movement. When it is openly discovered, it is as the pale form of Narcissus. Here, from Tennyson's *In Memoriam*,

> What find I in the highest place
> But mine own phantom chanting hymns

is an emphasis quite unlike the assured and sustained significance of the 'I' at the time of its formation. Here it is a literariness and not a literature, since it dwells in borrowed resources. Its endemic absorption generates an inevitable dialectic: the steady attenuation of the selfhood causes in turn an attenuation of the outward reality to which it clings. As the personality becomes more decadent, so the world assumes a dream-like and only semi-substantial form. The connection here is between the poetry of Tennyson and the finely observed but insubstantial world of pre-Raphaelite painting and verse.

'I' can only achieve an identity by divorcing itself from itself, by objectifying itself in a context somewhat more solid than its own 'individuality'. Browning creates dramatic personae within his monologues, for example, who place themselves in a world of exterior truths; they are not the interpreters (as they would be in the writing of Nietzsche) but the true voices of 'good' and 'evil', 'nature' and 'god'. And if there is one general meaning that unites the otherwise disparate works of Morris, Browning, Tennyson and Meredith, it is the new morality of art. General truths of religion and society sanctify their troubled art, and lend it value. If the romantic 'I' once seemed close to overturning the featureless language of socialised truths, it now returns to affirm it. There is once again a content:

> Knowledge comes, but wisdom lingers, and I linger on the shore
> And the individual withers, and the world is more and more.

And this, from Tennyson's *Locksley Hall*, is published one year before Mallarmé's *Les Poésies*. In England, there is no literature but rather a continuing rhetoric of social truths. The epiphany of language within Mallarmé's work excises the 'I' of moral experience; in England, it persists without interrogation and finds rest only by creating a landscape of truths and concealing itself there:

> I have feet on my native land, I am one with my kind
> I embrace the purpose of God, and the doom assigned.

This flat and denotative language carries over into the first years of our own century, and the Edwardian and Georgian establishment persists without question in the values of the nineteenth century. It is the time of Galsworthy, Stephen Moore's *Defence of Common Sense* (remember the origin of that 'common' sense) and Bloomsbury. In contrast, there was an unease and diversity in European cultural life of the same period, since it was the moment of Cubism and Futurism. In England, the dominant tone is still liberal, anti-theoretical and humane; the seventeenth-century values upon which this tone is based became more and more transparent until they left only a residue of familiar truths which survived by being decorative. This would be of simply historical interest, were it not that one of the few major innovations of the period was the establishment of 'English studies' in the universities. The tone of the age still leaves its imprint here, since it was precisely that humane and practical culture which was defined and indeed institutionalised within 'English studies'—and it is the one which persists into our own time.

But it would be quite wrong to impose a uniformity of thought and response upon the period. There did exist a self-conscious spirit of modernism, but it existed in writers who did not so much want to create a 'new' literature as to revive significant features of an earlier one. The central text here is of course Pound's *Personae*, which was published in 1909, in the depths of Edwardianism. It is a work which very clearly suffers all the tensions of a writing uneasy within the pervasive orthodoxy of the time and yet unable to make the purely general and aesthetic transition of the European writers. I could adduce here the contemporaneous attempt of D. H. Lawrence to construct a myth out of private, sensory consciousness, or the attempt of Yeats to mould the selfhood into an emblem: theirs is the most radical work of the time,

34

but their affiliations are with the romantic tradition and its reification of the self. And since the tradition, at that late date, could sustain itself only in a generalised and public context, theirs is a writing which is necessarily self-willed and self-justifying. There is something of this in the poetry of Pound.

A first reading of *Personae* suggests Pound's connection with the Victorians, and specifically with the work of Browning and D. G. Rossetti, but his poetry is not decorative or derivative in the Georgian mode. Pound uses a range of traditions and of sources to develop a verse much clearer and much more assured than that of his contemporaries. His fastidious attention to metrics serves to increase its power:

> I suppose there are a few dozen verities
> That no shift of mood can shake from us:
>
> One place where we'd rather have tea
> (Thus far hath modernity brought us)
> "Tea" (Damn you!)

The language here uses the inflection of a colloquial voice to such an extent that it is generally referred to as a 'voice', but if it is a voice it is not one that preserves 'experience'—that set of moral relations to which it is generally aligned. Pound puts it this way in *Vorticism*: "I began this search for the real in *Personae*, casting off complete masks of the self in each poem." "Personae" were the masks of classical actors, and each poem is the mask of a tradition through which the poet speaks, continually acquiring different identities in the task of creating a multiform role. Yeats also referred to his "masks", and both poets share the attempt to affirm a poetic voice without rooting it in the personal and so having to confront its orthodox origin; for Pound, this origin does not lie within certain seventeenth-century, or even nineteenth-century texts, but rather in certain European works, particularly those of the medieval poets and of Heinrich Heine. Pound breaks with the pervading Anglo-Saxon tradition in the sense that the 'I' which he adopts is not that of moral experience, but is in fact the combined voice of earlier poetry. It is this which constitutes his particular modernism: he reclaims the selfhood for English poetry by establishing it upon units of discourse. The 'I' then becomes a literature, since it is "about nothing" except itself. Here is a passage from *Hugh Selwyn Mauberly*:

> His true Penelope was Flaubert,
> He fished by obstinate isles
> Observed the elegance of Circe's hair
> Rather than the mottoes on sun-dials.
>
> Unaffected by the "march of events",
> He passed from man's memory in l'an trentiesme
> De son eage; the case presents
> No adjunct to the Muses' diadem.

The purity of line here transcends personal or demotic variation. Its precision and resonance confirm that sense of other, and earlier writings being folded into one speech. It is not the language which emerges into its own space here, as it is in Mallarmé, but a specifically poetic tradition of the voice. The poetry here has the outwardness and presence of *speech* (to be distinguished from Mallarmé's *writing*), but a speech which has excised the temporary contours of experience and subjective truth: it is as if subject could become object. But Pound still dwells within the language of the selfhood even in the act of objectifying it, and it is no accident that Anglo-Saxon modernism cannot reach beyond this dualism. And if there is to be one constant theme, it is this continual resurgence of the personal.

Pound's particular literariness was not followed by his contemporaries, however, and at the centre of the English poetry of the period there is a troubled regard for tone and private voice which had already vanished from the main European texts. And the Vorticist movement, of which Pound was a member, is an apt example of the persistence of these conventional values, since it is a paradoxical resurgence of traditionalism which marks this most radical of Anglo-Saxon movements. It was unique in its combination of poets, such as Pound, critics, such as Wyndham Lewis, and artists, like Henry Wadsworth and Gaudier-Brzeska, in an England which generally shows a divergence of creative activity. It was a unique movement, too, in its recognition of contemporary European culture: its magazine, *Blast* (published in 1914), has in this sense a significance analogous to that of the writings of Coleridge and Arnold. The peculiar verve of the magazine has the spirit of the Futurist journals of the period, and some of the paintings of Henry Wadsworth, for example, emphasise the pervasive debt to the Cubist movement in Paris. This kind of resourcefulness shows up to best effect in the critical writings of *Blast*, the only ones which try to recognise and analyse the European achievement. But this is to say everything that can be said, since the Vorticists' actual intellectual debt to the French and Italian movements is one which goes largely unacknowledged. The important critical borrowings are elsewhere, since the critical emphasis of the English group rests largely on the work of the German expressionists—particularly on what were considered to be the "organic" and "spiritual" forms of such painters as Kandinsky. It was this spirit which best suited their strongly indigenous stance.

Blast saw itself as a purely national force: "We are against Europeanism, the abasement of the miserable intellectual before anything coming from Paris." And "England is just now the most favourable country for the appearance of great art". This, and the strong anti-intellectualism, are familiar cries in this country. Wyndham Lewis gives it a contemporary context in his polemic against Picasso's late cubism, where Lewis anticipates a return to a kind of "naturalism" deriving from German expressionism and its drive towards a "unity of form". These names have appeared before, in the criticism of Coleridge and of Arnold, since they are the guise of a humanist aesthetic.

The Vorticists concentrate upon that, by now in this analysis characteristically, English sense of the individual: "*Blast* presents an Art of the Individual." It was in this context, of course, that Pound reclaimed the selfhood for his poetry. And again, "The nearest thing in England to a great traditional French artist is a great revolutionary English one", where the distinction rests upon a sense of the power of Anglo-Saxon individualistic workmanship. It is ironic that their 'revolution' could not be more traditional. It is no accident that their prose closely resembles that of William Blake; there is even a prose poem in *Blast*, entitled *Hamp*, which draws heavily upon Blake's prophetic books. In fact, the position of Blake in the eighteenth century—and, I might add, that of John Bunyan at the time of the first modernism—is typical of each English literary revolution. A counter-mythology is constructed, a kind of anti-language to the culture: it is a wholly new system of truths in Blake's writing, and in the work of Bunyan it is a mythology of the Word which counters the rational and transparent discourse of the first modernism. They were both convinced that their work derived from a tradition and a vocabulary of moral thought much older than the one in which they happened to find themselves. Both writers (a later example might be Lawrence) were 'revolutionary' in the sense that they conceived of themselves as traditionalists, as more profoundly orthodox than their contemporaries. This has been the general principle of English literary revolutions.

And it is also the context of the Vorticists' plea "for LIFE, a new living Abstraction", which can only refer to a vague humanism and an even vaguer concept of the selfhood. The Vorticists are as anti-theoretical as their Edwardian counterparts, and their distinctive achievement is only that of the synthesis of conflicting trends. It is strongly national while at the same time resembling the European avant-garde, since it remains essentially an appeal to an orthodox spirit of 'individuality' which had already passed from the French and Italian writers. Which passed, more precisely, with the advent of Dada. This is a movement which began in 1914, at the same time as Vorticism; a comparison of the two movements will help to clarify the general contrast and the permanent distinction between Anglo-Saxon and European culture.

Dada can be seen as a symptom of general historical collapse, and as part of that pessimism generated by the Great War and by the dislocation of the classical universe in the work of Einstein and Planck. Dada is nihilistic and iconoclastic in a specifically political sense, but its position is more complicated than any simply historical one. It was an eclectic movement, bringing together Arp, Tzara, Picabia, Stieglitz, Schwitters and Man Ray, and it was also an international one, appearing separately in Zurich, Berlin, Paris and New York. It rejects the past, and the future; it rejects classical art, contemporary art, and the idea of art. It seems to have emerged by accident and then to have disappeared without trace. But Dada lives; it is connected to the movement of European modernism and it is necessary for its progress. Unlike the Vorticist movement, it was able to make an effective statement because it continues that interrogation of artistic form which had been begun by Nietzsche and Mallarmé.

The earlier analysis of their writing had confirmed the emergence of language within it, a language which is trying to achieve the permanence and autonomy of natural objects. The Cubists, the direct predecessors of Dada, trace a similar path in their absorption in the form of painting. Their vision shifts from figural and representational art, to a theoretical decision to paint or present the shallowness and two-dimensionality of the picture-plane itself. But, as was recognised in the poetry of Mallarmé, this movement of art to describe itself beyond 'meaning' or perspective, the painterly equivalent of meaning, casts its own nature into doubt. Dada rises out of this troubled interrogation of form, but it rids itself of the latent ambiguity by transforming its context. On one level Dada is in fact a sustained attack upon the privileged status, the individualised 'presence', of the art object. Its use of 'found' natural materials in the painting, and the use of random selection in the writing, does not destroy the creative nature of these activities. It simply denies them the name of 'art', and denies the fact that they possess any distinctive qualities which are not simply our own projection of ourselves. 'Art' is the transformation of the natural world through the intervention of men, but if it can attain the status of a natural object it ceases to be mediated through man and is no longer 'art'. This is the power of Dada: it denies "us". The dialectic which the Dadists establish between their work and the concept of art is, in fact, a dialectic within humanism itself and its aesthetic.

Marcel Duchamp is the most significant force within Dada, in the sense that it is he who brings its theoretical content into the light. His *Nude Descending A Staircase* was exhibited at the New York Armory Show in 1913, and his career from that point combines a series of public gestures which now constitute a total, but generally unacknowledged, statement. At the centre of his work stand the "Readymades", the found and already finished objects which Duchamp ironically describes as his 'art'. There is the urinal, for example, and "in New York in 1915 I bought at a hardware store a snow shovel on which I wrote 'in advance of the broken arm' ". Duchamp sometimes reverses this process to demonstrate the simplicity of his equation: he will turn a Rembrandt into an ironing board. Art has finally attained the status of a natural object which, according to Duchamp, it has always been seeking. It is altogether de-mystified (by being altogether de-humanised), and Duchamp makes a break with the cultural tradition as radical as that of Cezanne or of Nietzsche. The ease with which it is achieved says less about the work of Duchamp than it does about the precarious character of the creative values of humanism and individualism. A sentence of Duchamp's sets the appropriate context: ". . . these pieces are visually indifferent, with a total absence of good or bad taste." This is exactly the point: they exist outside the aesthetic sphere. Duchamp takes the activity of his European predecessors a stage further, and displaces the aesthetic category entirely. Why this should be important, and how it connects with the earlier displacement of humanism in the writings of Mallarmé and Nietzsche, are questions which now have to be resolved.

It is generally assumed that 'aesthetics', like 'literature' and 'experience', is part of a family of concepts which has always been with us. But it has become a commonplace of this analysis that all of these concepts have a source and a chronology, and that to discover them is to reveal the ground on which we still walk. The name of 'aesthetics', for example, appears in 1735 in the *Reflections* of Alexander Baumgarten. It is actually established at the end of Baumgarten's study: "As our definition is at hand, a precise designation can easily be devised. The Greek philosophers and the Christian fathers have already carefully distinguished between things perceived (αἰσθητα) and things known (νοήτα). It is entirely evident that they did not equate things known with things of sense, since they honoured with this name things also removed from sense (therefore images). Therefore things known are to be known by the superior faculty as the object of logic; things perceived are to be known by the inferior faculty, as the object of the science of perception, or *aesthetics*."

40

Baumgarten is discussing the provenance of poetry here, and it is clear that the art-work is being identified as the object of sensuous cognition: the context is that of orthodox rationalism, since perception is described as the "lower part of the cognitive faculty" giving place to "reason" and its relations. Aesthetics is to be secondary to logic, and is to exist within its space; Baumgarten uses a deductive mode, for example, in his presentation of aesthetics, and analyses the "lucid order" of the poem. The principles of aesthetics are to be those of harmony, clarity and distinctiveness. The empirical perception of the art-work is formulated in these terms, since it is the understanding which exercises its ordering functions upon the experience. The birth of the perceptualist interpretation of art is, in fact, the fulfilment of classical rationalism since it can now be mediated through the natural world. This is the horizon of aesthetics.

And since aesthetics is a branch of rationalism, it is to be dedicated to an image of the unity of man. The rational self defines itself, and affirms its integrity, by presenting an *other*: the understanding creates the lower, aesthetic faculty and thus extends the range of its judgements. Man raises himself as a subject, so creating a world of objects—in this case, art objects—which are presented to him. The values which he ascribes to those objects are necessarily his own values, and so it is that he creates a human culture and a cultural tradition. Aesthetics affirms an art which has been divested of its transcendental content, and which has been turned into an instrument of man's satisfaction by embodying those rational values which he thinks of as peculiarly his own. The art object becomes humanised and useful, and a blind humanism develops—"Nothing is beautiful except man alone: all aesthetics rests upon this naïvete, which is its first truth," as Nietzsche saw it. And the naïvete actually appears in such texts as Lipp's *Abstraktion und Einfuhlung*: "The beautiful object harmonises with man's faculties. Man feels at one with the object. In it he discovers himself." This touchstone of value is exactly the one which changed language into a vehicle for human and social 'truths' at the time of the first modernism.

A classic formulation of these 'truths' appears in Burke's *Essay On The Sublime and Beautiful* since, despite the essay's apparent transition from strictly rational values, it prescribes a humanism and an aesthetic utilitarianism which were to be taken up by Coleridge and Arnold. For Burke, the two central human instincts are those of social cohesiveness and self-preservation, and it is the prerogative of art to substantiate them both. The beautiful object creates a harmony between man and the work, thus affirming a community of values which rests upon man. Art is the mediatress between man and the natural world. The sublime, on the other hand, depends upon the lack of harmony and excites a prospect of pain or danger which strengthens my hold upon, and delight in, my rational self. These are familiar statements, but they bear repeating here in order to confirm the essential continuity of Anglo-Saxon cultural values, since the tenor of these claims is taken up by Coleridge and by Arnold. The art object is somehow secondary in what is essentially a statement about individual and social value. Art possesses a humane purpose.

The other major aesthetic statement is that of Kant in his *Critique of Judgement*, and all subsequent aesthetics (up to the point of its deconstruction in the work of Duchamp) has moved between the opposing formulations of Kant and Burke. Kant argues against the humanistic assumptions of Burke's *Essay* by asserting, for the first time, that the beautiful is the object of an entirely disinterested satisfaction: art "has the mere form of purposiveness, without purpose". It bears no relation to any ethical concept, and so for Kant it has no human utility and embodies no human perfection. What kind of experience, then, is 'aesthetic'? It cannot be a cognitive judgement, since aesthetics is a name "by which we understand that whose determining ground is no other than subjective". The realm of subjectivity, which aesthetics celebrates, is not implicated in matters of external use or purpose, but is indifferent and free within itself: ". . . in saying it is beautiful and in showing that I have taste, I am concerned not with that in which I depend on the existence of the object, but with that which I make out of this representation in myself . . . I am indifferent as regards the existence of the object." These last phrases are the most forceful of all, since for Kant aesthetic satisfaction consists in a subjective awareness of the harmony between the imaginative representation and the understanding: in other words, it is an affirmation of pure mind, and distinct from the body and its existence.

The cognitive faculties exist in free play by means of the art object, and this is what Kant means by purposiveness without purpose. It is a formal purposiveness, in which "noumenal" relations display themselves outside the boundaries or moral and practical experience, thus remaining perfectly articulate and complete. What is experienced by the aesthetic faculty is the uncorrupted relations of the noumenal world. Aesthetics, then, affirms the delight in pure rationality and in so doing confirms the sphere of pure and 'use-less' subjectivity.

But both Kant and Burke, whether it be one's version of subjectivity or the other's version of humanism, continue the divisions of a higher 'thought' as opposed to a lower 'perception', and it is these which Duchamp overturns in his exhibiting the urinal and the bicycle-wheel as 'art'. The Greek αἴσθησις makes the sensuous foundation of aesthetics very clear, but Duchamp says that he chose his objects for their "visual indifference". And that is the point: Duchamp abolishes the perceptual basis of his art. It is his own anaesthetic. These works are "beyond good or bad taste" because they cannot be considered at the level of subjective and perceptual judgement, but rather at the level of a general statement about the nature of art. The Readymades have no inner lucidity or sensuous proportion, and we are no longer in Burke's world of human purpose or Kant's world of imaginative appreciation. A new distance is created between man and object, since the object can no longer be interpreted as a mode of our being.

So by abolishing the aesthetic category, Duchamp is able to confuse the Cartesian separation of faculties into 'higher' and 'lower'. His is not an art which appeals either to sense or to reason as separate categories, since it is not one which can be organised to suit man's need for harmony and control. The Dadaist poet, Jean Arp, puts the point in another context in On My Way: "I became more and more removed from aesthetics . . . I wanted to find another order, another value for man in nature. He was no longer to be the measure of all things, no longer to reduce everything to his own measure." Dada thus transcends the social and utilitarian assumptions of the humanist aesthetic, and it may be relevant to note here the speed with which Dada took to film: like film, Dada is anti-contemplative and, again like film, it destroys any sense of a 'tradition'.

But Duchamp's destruction of aesthetics as the mediator of the art-object has at its side the mysteriousness and invisibility of Duchamp himself. The overturning of art as a simply human phenomenon entails the overturning of the metaphysics of 'presence' within the object, of what is unique and private. The concept of individual creation, by means of which art becomes a paradigm of moral experience, is one that necessarily vanishes. Duchamp's withdrawal parallels and completes the withdrawal of Mallarmé from his writings, and the idea of artistic 'personality' steadily declines. The bicycle wheel and the urinal are authorless and now forgotten works, since they existed only as statements. But what becomes of *homo humanus*, who can no longer find himself in art or in discourse? Does he simply reappear as a category in the social sciences?

This relation between the now intangible self and the authorless object is one that has not yet resolved itself. In the course of this analysis there will be a recurrence of certain key positions, which suggests a continual re-appraisal of a situation which was already present in the first two decades of this century and which has yet to advance: modernism, however we come to define it, does not have a simple or necessary chronology. Of course this tension is one that is never established in England, where the concept of artistic personality seems as permanent and as secure as ever. The aesthetic humanism of Coleridge and Arnold is carried over into our own century without interrogation, and it is this spirit which pervades the founding of English studies in the universities. The English School at Cambridge, for example, which had Sir Arthur Quiller-Couch as its first guide and spokesman, is an interesting case of how that spirit developed and prospered.

The text of Quiller-Couch's inaugural address to the English school, in 1913, repeats all of the familiar emphases we have read elsewhere. The address opens with an extensive reference to Plato, and its whole context becomes a classical one since it is only in reference to a rhetorical version of the past that Quiller-Couch can formulate and defend certain truths. "Literature" be-

comes part of a humane "tradition" and is brought within the
sphere of orthodox values: Plato and the ancient tragedians exem-
plify certain human "truths", and their texts have become a storehouse of recorded values. And of course "literature is a nurse of
noble natures, and right reading makes a full man;" this is only
a short step from the later criticism of two jewels of the Cambridge English school, F. R. Leavis and Raymond Williams. For
Quiller-Couch, language is instrumental: it "improves our sensibility" by embodying certain moral values. But where are these
values to be found? Where else, in our culture, but in the "individual". It is the characteristic stance of our humanism, and for
Quiller-Couch "we read with minds intent on discovering just what
the author's mind intended". He puts the point more clearly in his
On A School of English: "Literature being so personal a thing,
you cannot understand it until you have some personal understanding of the men who wrote it." That sense of the 'individual'
emerges here as is it were a universally received truth.

It is part of the "tradition" which Quiller-Couch addresses himself to. But of what else does the tradition consist? Quiller-Couch
gives a little encomium to Sainte-Beuve at the end of his inaugural address, in which he describes him as "the representative
critic", and if we place this beside Matthew Arnold's similar praise
of the French critic a shared sense of the "tradition" emerges. The
Cambridge English school was, for Quiller-Couch, the institution-
alisation of the tones and attitudes of Sainte-Beuve. It was meant
to embody that public, semi-classical manner; it was to be concerned with the "individual" and the "personal". But what is of
most significance, and what comes to mark the study of English
in the universities, is Sainte-Beuve's and, by extension, Quiller-
Couch's disdain for any kind of theoretical enquiry. Quiller-Couch
puts it this way in his address: "Our investigations will deal largely
with style . . . aiming at the concrete, eschewing all general
definitions and theories."

This is the orthodox ground of all "practical criticism" and
"keeping to the text" generalities which still plague the study of
literature, but our own analysis of modernism throws Quiller-
Couch's key sentence into a different light: the concept of what
is "concrete" and "solid" has been found to be no less a general-

ity than anything which has succeeded it. It appeared at the time of the first modernism, along with such concepts as "simple" and "useful", and Quiller-Couch's criticism rests upon that attenuated empiricism, that sense of "common sense", the origins of which I have already outlined. It is paradoxical that a school of 'literature' should be established in a culture which does not recognise the force or context of literature, and that it should be founded upon a philosophical tradition which had already been overturned in Europe—despite that school's pretensions to a classical, European spirit. These are the fruits of that failure to respond to "general definitions and theories", the attention to which initiated the modern movement in France, Germany and Italy.

3

The Uses of Language

Language, most dangerous of possessions, has been given to Man.
                                                        Hölderlin

Sticks and stones may break my bones, but words will never hurt me.

This study has arrived, chronologically, at the works of Eliot and Joyce although they both seem a world away from the Edwardian dispensation. Their exilic writing has come to constitute our particular modernism, principally because it has been seen to be one of discontinuity and ambiguity after the bland self-certainty of Edwardian texts. It is not surprising that the critics who proclaim what is 'modern' and what is not should do so in terms of content or tone, since this is the general way of looking at the object. But it may be possible to read Eliot and Joyce in another context, and it may by a reading that separates what is tangential from what endures.

Eliot's *Prufrock* is the poem of a young man. It was published in 1917, and is generally regarded as the precursor to what today is 'modern'; it seems to be ironic, elliptical and it uses a range of demotic imagery to gain effects that would have previously been implausible:

> I have measured out my life with coffee spoons

But this order of change is only the most apparent, because it is the one most easily borrowed or imitated. Another analysis might proceed instead from the ubiquitous 'I' which opens the poem:

> Let us go then, you and I,
> While the evening is spread out against the sky. . . .

> I should have been a pair of ragged claws
> Scuttling across the floors of silent seas.

The range of effects here is obviously original; Pound's *Mauberly*
was published only three years later, and yet the persona in Eliot's
poem is much more substantial and much more elusive. It is
elusive because it has no central point and no fixed position. It is
an indirect voice which, like that of Nietzsche for example, can
create a wealth of tones and meanings by not being definitive in
an orthodox sense. It has a strength of tone and allusion because
(and here again there is a parallel with Nietzsche's 'I') it is located
within the contours and recesses of an inherited language. This is
the literary past which shines on the surface of all Eliot's poetry:
I could put the point differently by noting that the voice of
Pound is the voice of purified speech, but for Eliot the voice is that
of the inherited writing.

In Eliot we respond to a language that is ironically full and
achieved despite the apparent sense of lamentation:

> Shall I part my hair behind? Do I dare to eat a peach?
> I shall wear white flannel trousers, and walk upon the beach.
> I have heard the mermaids singing, each to each.
>
> I do not think that they will sing to me.

The movement of the line here, with its rhythmic assurance and
tonal harmonies, is not inflated or undercut by the 'I' of its progress: there is no subject to circumscribe the line or its particular
resonance. Unlike Yeats, for example, Eliot does not conduct
an argument outside the language of the poem and no generalised
selfhood is imposed upon it. The various textures and multiple
reminiscences of the language exist beside the peevish and worried
voice of the poem; the 'I' is mediated through an assured writing
so that it displays an internal consistency and an aesthetic or
sensuous harmony which derive as much from a literary context,
in Eliot's allusiveness, as they do from Eliot's superb technical proficiency. But why is it, then, the voice of lamentation? Why does
this 'I', at the level of content, seem vitiated and defenceless?

> I grow old . . . I grow old. . . .
> I shall wear the bottoms of my trousers rolled.

There is a trace here of the orthodox 'I' of moral experience, but it is one that is achieving objectivity and substance only through the form of the language: the persona takes as its mask, in fact, the inherited autonomy of language itself. I could put it differently by noting that the self is attached to exactly that entity which exists beyond the self and its relations, and that this accounts for its peculiarly disembodied tone. It is the overt technical order of the poem, and the literary tradition of which it is a part, that locate the voice and yet at the same time displace it: giving it that plangency within the harmonic certainties of the line.

Eliot has achieved here something very different from his contemporaries, who postulate the selfhood only on private and derivative terms. He establishes the permanence and autonomy of language within the poem, thus both undercutting and lending a new form of substantiality to its persona. J. Alfred Prufrock is a voice, a name that laments the formal proficiency of its own statements. It resides in the poetry as a formal device, as a zone for expression, but one that recognises itself as such and manages to retain a tenuous and somewhat ironic hold upon the 'experience' which language is displacing. The analysis of this tension must be left incomplete, since Eliot dwells in its uncertainty; it is a tension that emerges in his later poetry, and it is in fact so central to his achievement that there is an elaboration of it (an elaboration, you might say, of *Prufrock*) in his collection of critical essays, *The Sacred Wood*, which was published in 1920.

In these essays Eliot attempts to order and to synthesise those tensions between language and subjectivity which generate the force of his early poetry. He sees the matter in a different context, in that of "personality" and "poetic form", but although the problem is unstated it is everywhere apparent. The most influential essay in the collection is 'Tradition and The Individual Talent', since it is the only theoretical enquiry into the poetic selfhood during the period; Eliot concerns himself with those issues which had been brought into prominence by Mallarmé and Duchamp—issues which were not faced or even recognised by Eliot's English contemporaries.

The most radical of Eliot's strategies in this essay lies in his awareness of the slightness of that selfhood which emerges through the language of poetry: "The poet has not a 'personality' to express, but a particular medium, which is only a medium and not a personality. . . . It is in this depersonalisation that art may be said to approach the condition of science. . . . Poetry is not the expression of personality, but an escape from personality." Eliot's concern here is for the medium of poetry, language; he questions the status of the selfhood and suggests that it is an improper concept to be introduced into the formal object. Eliot also seems aware of the dubious status of the private 'creator' of art, a concept which has more to do with economics of production than it does with the actual procedures of the poet. But there is, of course, a fundamental divergence between Eliot's position and that of the European modernists, and it appears in Eliot's notion of the poet's "escape" from personality: he is not described as "escaping" into, and celebrating language, but rather as "escaping" into a mysterious entity which is himself and yet not himself. It is something called "the new art emotion".

Eliot places great emphasis throughout the essay on the role of "emotions and feelings" in the creation of poetry. He describes "the structural emotion" of the drama and asserts that "the emotion in poetry will be a very complex thing". But however complex it may be, Eliot still insists on that aesthetic duality in which "feeling", as opposed to "thought", is the proper object of art. For Eliot, the "mind" of the poet is an invisible "catalyst" through which his individual feelings are combined and transformed into certain "universal" forms of emotion. Poetry is placed once again in an orthodox humanistic context: as a medium through which we can recognise a lucid and permanent image of ourselves. By conceiving of poetic language as the sensible instrument of complex qualities of "emotion", whether universal or not, Eliot persists in that rational aesthetic which Duchamp had overturned when he had denied that art is a paradigm of 'feelings' or 'experience'. But it is exactly that paradigmatic force which Eliot sustains in his assertion of the objectivity of "the new art emotion"; "the emotion of art is impersonal" but it reifies our selves. It is as if the poet could produce a science of feeling in which we might see our separate needs and faculties unified, and absolved from particularity; in this sense, Eliot's theory acts as an analogy to those exact studies which were even then appearing as the "science of human nature", the social sciences.

Eliot, then, engineers a simple alternative. He is aware of the dubious status of the private voice and its range of feeling, but he constructs as an alternative, not an autonomy of language, but an impersonal and a-temporal voice of feeling. What is the context for this "impersonal" feeling which is not grounded on an idea, however distantly derived, of the troubled self? For Eliot, it is constituted by the past of written literature. It is the "tradition" which may or may not be known to the "individual talent", but by which he is judged and of which he is a part: "The existing monuments form an ideal order among themselves, which is modified by the introduction of new works among them." It is very like that idea of a humane tradition which Arnold established, and which Quiller-Couch employed as the context of critical and moral values—and Eliot's support of this imaginary community explains in part his popularity with the academic establishment.

But what precisely is this "tradition"? Despite Eliot's attachment to the "medium" of poetry, it is not the Mallarmian sense of literature as a self-sustaining form emerging into consciousness. The idea of language does not present itself very clearly to Eliot, and for him it remains an instrument for communicating the objects and qualities of experience. Nor is his tradition at all like that of Nietzsche's history of multiple interpretation, since Eliot's criticism affirms the truth of certain certainties. No, his "tradition" is one of exactly those "impersonal emotions" it is supposed to create and to support. It is through the language of poetry that private feeling is changed into impersonal emotion, but the cause and context of this change is the tradition of impersonal emotion itself.

"Impersonal emotion", the relief of humanism after a long siege, is merely posited—just as the literary "tradition" itself exists without argument or justification. Nothing is questioned, and Eliot simply accepts the orthodox categories while changing their terms. The problem is that there is no new problem: the notion of the selfhood, although called into doubt, is simply reconstructed on other terms; the poem has the aesthetic categories

51

of exemplary feeling and formal unity imposed upon it; the nature of language is not discussed, and it remains an opaque and troubling entity which Eliot never explicitly confronts.

But only explicitly, since *The Waste Land* acquires much of its force from unacknowledged tension between language and orthodox 'meaning'. This poem is generally read in terms of a mythic or thematic structure, a kind of inner meaning which its fragments contain. And at one level the poem invites that response. But it may be more interesting to consider its exercise of language as one that implicity denies the realm of orthodox meaning. *The Waste Land* exists at maximum pressure in its employment of literary allusion and quotation, but the allusions are not there for their own sake. The literary context of Prufrock's voice has been deepened, and at the same time become more explicit:

> 'Oh keep the Dog far hence, that's friend to men,
> Or with his nails he'll dig it up again!
> You! hypocrite lecteur!—mon semblable,—mon frère!'

It is not necessary to read Eliot's notes to recognise the derivations here, but in their combination these words cease to be merely a collection of sources. There is something hallucinatory about this combination of diction and movement, and they have become a new thing. It is not that they possess a meaning which is the sum of their separate parts, nor that they embody the poet's own voice within a tradition of voices. The words have acquired their own density, and their force comes from differences of diction which, although staying in evidence, are mediated by the life of the whole. The source of this life is language itself. Eliot employs the language of ballads, direct quotation, pastiche, generalised commentary and narrative, and even rag-time:

> Why then Ile fit you. Hieronymo's mad againe.
> > It's so elegant
> > So intelligent

and each variety of language is given an autonomy, a proper life that exists beyond the customary Anglo-Saxon context of connotation and meaning. This is dramatised in the second section of *The Waste Land*, 'The Game of Chess', in which the sterility of the private voice ("What shall I do now? What shall I ever do?") is placed within the historical and mythological reminiscences of another language ("The Chair she sat in, like a burnished throne"). And it is language which speaks, and which becomes the hidden subject.

It necessarily remains hidden because Eliot still believes himself to be working within a world of denotation: not in the sense of a generalised theme or content, although critics naturally have discovered one, but of the connection of Eliot's language with the values of moral experience and subjectivity. But when this connection is explicitly asserted, the poetry fails. These are the last lines of *The Waste Land*:

> *Quando fiam uti chelidon*—O swallow swallow
> *Le Prince d'Aquitaine à la tour abolie*
> These fragments I have shored against my ruins
> Why then Ile fit you. Hieronymo's mad againe.
> Datta. Dayadhvam. Damyata.
>
> Shantih shantih shantih

The words have become loosened here, and they become detached from each other in a disciplined reading; the surface of the poetry does not have the syntactical concentration and harmonic force which shape the earlier passage. The language here is not autonomous, but stubbornly referential: it exists in a part-to-part relation with certain literary meanings, and is dominated by a personal mood. The continuity of this poetry is not mediated within the language itself, but is compelled by the force of local emotion and remains external.

To talk of its external features is of course to invoke those conventional concepts of "inner" meaning and "outer" expression, and this is the only way of locating the flatness and discontinuity of the passage. Language has been pressed into the service of Eliot's voice, since Eliot's orthodoxy is not his royalism or his classicism but his central commitment to a version of the self that asserts and laments. In *The Waste Land* it is the figure of Tiresias who acts as the inclusive human consciousness behind the language: "What Tiresias sees, in fact, is the substance of the

53

poem," as Eliot puts it in his notes and despite the progress of the poetry toward achieving a form of self-identity, the external context of the poem is still an aesthetic and subjective one. Why else should the poem terminate with the failure of language to convey anything but an individual sense of weakness and restriction, a sense which is actually derived from the collapse of language into the boundaries of the selfhood?

In Eliot's poetry, then, the conventional aesthetics of language creates an external meaning which exists in a state of tension with its proper autonomy. We read ourselves into the consciousness of "Tiresias", although the original self-certainty of the language had invited an act of self-transcendence. By the close of the poem, the poetry has been domesticated and we are offered an immediate human content without reflective consciousness:

> We think of the key, each in his prison,
> Thinking of the key, each confirms a prison.

Generalised meaning is conveyed in an attenuated language, which refers to a world of human "truth"; it is very bad poetry indeed. But it was this which spurred Eliot's popularity, and that sense of correspondence which his readers felt with his "description of a whole generation". His actual achievement was to go some way toward recognising the power of language when it becomes a literature, but this has naturally gone unnoticed.

Unnoticed or not, it places him beside that other figure of our modernism, James Joyce. *Ulysses* was published in the same year as *The Waste Land*. The writings are of course very different, but the difference is not one between poetry and prose but one between different degrees of freedom. Eliot still in part maintains language as an instrument of personal expression, but for Joyce the world only exists through the mediation of language. *Ulysses* is the comic epic of the word; it requires exegesis, while *The Waste Land* requires thematic interpretation. But if there is difference, there is also common ground: their particular modernism, and it is one which comes to be characteristic of Anglo-Saxon culture, lies in their creative discovery of the history of language. The acquisition of an historical consciousness, and a concomitant awareness of the relativity of literary style, are responsible for the power of certain areas of *The Waste Land* and is also the central perspective of *Ulysses*.

But how did this common consciousness develop, since their specifically historical awareness of language as an object having its own structure has only a marginal connection with the self-reflective literature of, for example, Flaubert? Condillac's etymology is the first to lend language a natural autonomy, by reconstructing its natural history from its supposed beginnings in speech. But it may be more illuminating to stay closer to those first decades of the nineteenth century, in texts contemporaneous with those of Flaubert, to recognise the steady development of the consciousness of language as a natural object with its own laws of growth and change, and to anticipate the work of our own modernists.

In this sense, Wilhelm von Humboldt is the first linguist to be possessed by the spirit of modernism. In a letter to Wolff in 1805, he asserts that "I believe I have discovered the art of using language as a vehicle by which to explore the heights, depths and the diversity of the whole world". In *Linguistic Variability and Intellectual Development*, published in 1836, Humboldt makes the central distinction between "language" and "languages": "language is the sum total of creations, as in each case different from what is uttered . . . it grows to an independent power." And it is in this context that Humboldt talks of the *innere sprachform* of a people, the language which embodies its life and relations. It is this radical conception of language that establishes the proper study of it as a natural object: that is, it is one that becomes accessible to the same analysis as the objects of natural science. To use the prevailing biological metaphor of the time, it obeys the laws of its own being. But its characteristics cannot be immediately displayed since its manner of production, according to Humboldt, "remains completely undetermined" and it possesses an "obscure, undisclosed depth". Man exists in an uneasy relation to this entity, for it is employed as his particular speech and yet at the same time it transcends that speech: "By the same act through which he spins out the thread of language, Man weaves himself into its tissues."

There is a central ambiguity here that invades the whole of Humboldt's description: it is in his grounding of language in speech. Clearly, "language possesses an evident spontaneity even if its inherent nature is simultaneously inexplicable". But it is inexplicable only because it is seen as deriving from that spontaneity. And as long as linguistics took speech as its paradigm (as the 'origin' of language), the ambiguity could not be resolved.

This becomes emphasised in August Schleicher's development of Humboldt's thesis. For, although he establishes language upon the patterns and the constituents of spontaneous speech, he describes in substantial terms the absoluteness and autonomy of a Language which excises any origin within the world of utterance. Language becomes a natural object that develops outside the history of human consciousness. In *Sprachvergleichende Untersuchungen*, published in 1848, Schleicher puts it that "language has the rule of unalterable natural laws which man's will and whim are powerless to change in any way". Language combines according to laws of signification and relation, which are conceived as universal: man is not seen as an agent in the formation of language, but is seen simply as that which grows into its principles of expression. This is, in fact, a formalised and somewhat prosaic equivalent to Nietzsche's invasive irony and Mallarmé's ambiguous poetry. So how can linguistics remain within the context and paradigm of speech, now that the primary texts of modernism are established solely upon the written language?

Ferdinand de Saussure, whom I will be analysing further in a later chapter, may suggest an answer. He first establishes the study of linguistics on enduring principles: "the . . . true and unique object of linguistics is language studied in and for itself" is the last sentence of his *Cours du Linguistique Générale*. And de Saussure moves toward recognising the exemplary status of the *written* language as the form of linguistic inquiry. The context in which he affirms the self-sufficiency and autonomy of language is that famous distinction between language ("langue") and speech ("parole"), and although he does not identify "langue" with the written form of language the resemblance very soon becomes clear. What is autonomous is the "sign" which exists in a completely arbitrary relation to the object, and the coherence of language exists in the differential relation between these signs; the crucial self-sufficiency of language is that it exists prior to speech and its relations. It is at this point that linguistics becomes the first scholarship of modernism.

Of course the writing of Joyce never touches directly upon this new discipline, but it becomes the prevailing spirit through which his texts gain their strength and their expansiveness. It is an intellectual development which, as we have seen, affects the quality of Eliot's work, although as a formal discipline it presumably remained unknown to him. The particular quality of the modernism of both writers lies in their historical consciousness; they are aware, more than anything else, of the past and the volume of language—and of the uses to which it could be put. They both employ literary allusiveness to reinforce their writing, although their intentions in doing so are very different. Where Eliot tries to dispose language within a new order, by constructing a formal meaning, Joyce resides on its surfaces. He has the original faculty of play, and the continual references to Shakespeare within *Ulysses* delineate a common force, that casting on and off of the varieties of language in order to release its vitality and its sacredness.

Ulysses is pre-eminently the Book. Its structural model is the Homeric epic, and its range is not that one day in Dublin but the whole literary tradition which begins with Homer and ends with Joyce. And this Book is, in a sense, our only literature since it represents the first and still the only consciousness of the form and autonomy of language. Joyce overturns the "tradition" which has been traced through Arnold and Quiller-Couch, simply by being the first writer to adequately express it. His is not at all the achievement of Mallarmé, since he doesn't offer us a language which finds its autonomy ultimately sterile. His is rather a rhetoric of invention and accumulation. Joyce rediscovers the forgotten and various past of language, and redeploys it with a sense of its complete mastery over any possible 'meaning'. He draws out its history in ways which bear some relation to the scholarship of the linguists, but with a style and verve that surpass their certainty of knowledge.

The 'being' of language is in fact an uninterrupted becoming of realities and meanings: Joyce's work has been seen to be dramatic, but never quite in that sense. Characters like Leopold Bloom and Stephen are comic personae, because they exist within the forces of a language that they can never completely understand. Language embodies the comic impulse in *Ulysses* with much the same force as that of Nature in Shakespearian comedy. Here is the narrative of a bar conversation, which ends with a biscuit box being flung at the departing Bloom. It is organised in a multiple focus—first, Homeric parody:

> And lo, as they quaffed their cup of joy, a godlike messenger came swiftly in, radiant as the eye of heaven, a comely youth. . . .

late romantic prose:

> Through the hush of air a voice sang to them, low, not rain, not leaves in murmur, like no voice of strings of reeds

scientific description:

> calculated to inevitably produce in the human subject a violent ganglionic stimulus of the nerve centres, causing the pores of. . . .

journalese:

> The last farewell was affecting in the extreme. From the belfries far and near the funereal deathbell tolled unceasingly. . . .

Biblical prose:

> And they rose in their seats, those twelve of Iar, and they swore by the name of Him who is from everlasting. . . .

and what we blindly call 'realistic' prose:

> Begob he drew his hand and made a swipe and let fly. Gob be near sent it into the county of Longford. The bloody nag. . . .

and all of these styles reflect upon the same scene. In a later section, Joyce parodies the history of prose style from Anglo-Saxon to Romantic narrative. His "characters" only exist within certain styles, and here is Gertie who can only appear in the discourse of conventional sentiment which inscribes her:

> Her very soul is in her eyes and she would give worlds to be in the privacy of her own familiar chamber, giving way to tears, she could have a good cry and relieve her pent-up feelings. . . .

This is very funny in its mixture of sentiment and vulgarity, and it is with something of a shock that we read that Gertie is a cripple:

it is a shock because it represents a sudden invasion of 'meaning' into a self-sustaining world of language. The central facts of *Ulysses* are these unambiguous and well-defined areas of discourse that do not impinge upon one another; there are no people, there are only monologues. There may be a "bar" where the words pass, and it may even be geographically located, but it is only the context of the narrative and not its content. The use of the multiple, historical perspectives of language (the use, in fact, of the tradition) releases the reader from a fixed time and place, so that he may appreciate the abilities of language itself.

This comes close to Joyce's stated affinity with scholastic philosophy, and his Thomist sense of the word as sacramental. He seems to dwell in that time before seventeenth-century modernism; language partakes of the material world which manifests the signs of its presence, it resides in the world and it embodies it. Language is that signifying force in which meanings congregate; it is a symbol to be meditated on and also an interpretation to be enacted. It does not have that seventeenth-century plainness which transmits solid and simple truths, since it contains the possibility of many levels of meaning. Joyce seems by indirection to have recovered this historical substance of language, and to have turned his Book into a comic version of ritual.

But *Ulysses* is a literature in the sense that Flaubert and Mallarmé had defined it, and so it has no assured or theological ground on which to rest. Once language has retrieved its history, it emerges as its only subject, it is literature, it is "about nothing". The subject of *Ulysses* is itself, in the endless recapitulation of forms and texts. These textual involutions do not create the integrity of any one style through which we could view the 'real', and if there is a tension between the areas of free invention and the continuing narrative, it is the indispensable condition for Joyce's writing. Unlike Eliot, he is aware of the variations of language and does not try to solidify it and create a style from the tradition which would be 'his'.

It is paradoxical that both Joyce and Flaubert, who create a literature, should at various times have been described as aesthetes —when it is in fact they who finally dispel the aesthetic illusion, the illusion that there is a single style to which we respond as the 'true' and 'beautiful'. It has become evident, as a result of the work of Flaubert and Joyce, that the only kind of writing which is substantial is that which reveals itself as relative. Gertrude Stein, for example, wished to be modern and became merely contemporary. She adapted from film a kind of experimental writing in which language is stretched out into an endless reel of meaning: "A continuous present is a continuous present. I made almost a thousand pages of a continuous present." But the language is fixed at only one level, in a process of free association and 'presentness'; it tries to segregate itself from other forms of writing, and to claim for itself a private authenticity and special meaning. It turns itself, in fact, into an aesthetic phenomenon. The American 'realists' may seem markedly different but they took up a similar position, and Dos Passos or Dreiser remain aesthetes in their depiction of social reality. They create a naturalistic or reportorial style, mediating objects and facts, which is as specialised and as relative as any other: but for them, it is *the* language of fiction, and by reifying it they make it aesthetic. Their style prefigures and controls their ostensible content, since that transparent, 'natural' prose through which facts are mechanically transmitted is one which actually forms their vision of a suffocating material world: all that the style can present is the stubborn objectness and factuality of things.

Joyce has no single or simple vision of that kind. He uses reportorial techniques, and even newspaper typography, but only in order to describe the kind of world which is fabricated by those means. And he uses 'realistic' speech patterns and monologues in order to construct a vision of the day as it exists for the private consciousness:

> Say you never see them with three colours. Not true. That half-tabby-white-tortoiseshell in the City Arms with the letter em on her forehead. Body fifty different colours. Howth a while ago amethyst. Glass flashing. That's how that wise man what's his name with the burning glass. Then the heather goes on fire. It can't be tourists' matches. What?

But this private consciousness, with its fragments of memory and meaning, is obviously not the repository of meaning in *Ulysses*;

the aureate and technical periods of much of the rest of the prose could not derive from all this detail and cliché. I could put it another way by suggesting that writing does not emerge from speech, or from the individual, but only from other writing.

It is ironic that, with *Ulysses*, Anglo-Saxon modernism should emerge some fifty years after its European renaissance, and that it should develop during a period of European decadence. It is part of the essential ambiguity and frailty of the modern movement that it should have only brief periods of creative force, and we can in fact locate the beginning of its decline in the Surrealistic movement. Two years after the publication of *The Waste Land* and *Ulysses*, André Breton published in Paris the first *Manifesto of Surrealism*. Its themes are all too familiar after the polemics of Dada—"Surrealism asserts our complete non-conformism" but the central purpose of the movement is very different from that of Dada. It predates Joyce and even Eliot.

Surrealism claims an allegiance with the writings of Sigmund Freud ("We must give thanks to Sigmund Freud") in its general polemic against capitalism, and in the name of "the imagination perhaps on the point of reasserting itself, of reclaiming its rights" against "the realistic attitude, inspired by positivism". The claim for imaginative liberation here has nothing whatever to do with the Dadaistic overturning of all humane values, since the Surrealists claim for themselves a new art which is to be established upon a new image of man. Their "imagination" ransacks the familiar world in order to uncover hidden correspondences and symbols, and in order to refurbish those visionary acts which exist in childhood and in dreams. The Surrealists are trying to retrieve that conventional idea of the 'unity' of man, on much the same terms as it was established in the writings of humanism. Surrealist art is to be "useful" since poetry is "a name of getting out, a tool ideally suited to breaking certain limits". Poetry returns to its old status as a human agent, in the same gesture as the idea of Man returns to consciousness: "Au centre du monde est l'homme" writes Masson in *VVV*, the Surrealist magazine. In fact, for Breton, Surrealism becomes a political and humanistic movement; he became aligned with an orthodox Marxism—that is, with a version

C

of exactly that social positivism which had been explicitly rejected in appeals to the free "imagination".

All that is 'new' in Surrealism is Breton's invention of automatic writing, a state of passivity which evokes written thought. The attempt is being made to seize "la matière première" of language, whose images and symbols exist below the level of individual consciousness in a sort of collective unconscious. But there is a permanent distinction to be drawn between Surrealist theory and Surrealistic practice. It is a dichotomy which they actually set up themselves, by making public and accessible one dimension of Freudian theory while at the same time creating a poetry of thoroughly conventional qualities. Here is a sequence from Eluard:

> Une sublime chaleur bleue
> S' appuie aux tempes des fenêtres
> Belle alignée de plumes jusqu'aux limbes
> La parfumée la rose adulte le pavot et la fleur vierge de la torche
> Pour composer la peau enrobée de femmes nues

The difficulty and complexity of the poetry rests only on the alignments of its syntactical surface; the language is itself bland and harmonious, and can create its effects only by technical disjunctions. The imagistic and rhythmic potential are those of a conventional pastoral kind, deriving in part from Apollinaire's lyricism and further back, and the writing is 'aesthetic' in the sense that it returns to nineteenth-century symbolist texts without lending them a fresh access of strength. It is much like symbolist painting, which abandons the cubist interrogation of space and becomes once again representational, with an image of man and his desires at its centre. And it is this same orthodox spirit in Surrealist cinema: the films of Dali and Bunuel, for example, represent a wholly private reality. They create images of dream and eroticism which, because of their subjective origin, remain flat and conventional.

The central purpose of the Surrealist movement is to invest subjectively with a fresh kind of significance, by founding it upon universal principles. It is no longer defined, of course, in the orthodox contexts of reason or 'primary imagination', but in the

62

then fashionable terms of the Freudian 'unconscious'. Freud's actual achievement is not in question here, only the uses to which it was put. The idea of the 'unconscious' was rapidly becoming popularised and debased, until it came to represent the medium of universal truth and 'reality' (there was a vogue, for example, for such crass techniques as "stream of consciousness"). Conventional habits of thought are simply transferred into a new context. For the Surrealists, the unconscious becomes the ground of a poetic selfhood which can unite Man and invest humanism with a new significance. The fact that this entails the fracture of modernism, with its interrogation of the selfhood and of language, is clear enough: and the unconscious becomes the repository of cliché. "La matière première" of language is designed to suit certain kinds of human truth and so, like the earlier "universal grammar", becomes a debased and transparent currency. The progress of modernism is neither easy nor inevitable.

4

The Uses of the Self

Shall I go off to South America
Shall I put out in my ship to sea
Or get in my cage and be lions and tigers
Or—shall I be only Me?
    A. A. Milne: *When We Were Very Young*

One never loves anybody, one only loves qualities.
                   Pascal

The marks of subjectivity have been appearing throughout this analysis, but principally as that formal entity which exists in relation to language—whether disclosing it or in turn being concealed by it. I have traced its persistence within the Anglo-Saxon cultural tradition and its virtual disappearance within European modernism, although it declined there only to reappear under a different guise in Surrealism. It has in a sense merely been posited: as an extension of Cartesian syntax, for example, or as a remnant of the Romantic selfhood. But its context has never simply been that of language, and it does, in fact, undergo its own transformation in the movement of modernism.

The principal work here is, of course, that of Søren Kierkegaard. His is the first affirmation of subjectivity within the period of this study. In *Concluding Unscientific Postscript* he states that "in our age men had forgotten what it means to EXIST, and what INWARDNESS signifies" and it is in this context that Kierkegaard can make a break, as substantial as that of Nietzsche's affirmation of "interpretation" and "difference", with all previous knowledge. Like Nietzsche, his polemic is directed against what he calls "objective" and "world-historical" knowledge; Kierkegaard is the first to locate subjectivity outside the realm of systematic truths, and the first to suggest that it has a life radically distinct from such truths. All previous constructions of the self had been formed within a framework of truths that claimed objectivity and universality, whether it be the Cartesian *cogito* or the imaginative 'unity' which Coleridge affirms. The self was projected by idealistic theory as a mode of evidence. It was fixed in a realm of permanence and truth beyond sensory experience and its relations; the soul or subject-being was treated as separate, and as affirming an absolute form of being. But Kierkegaard, again with an unmistakable similarity to Nietzsche, evokes another world: "existence is a process of becoming," and he is able to overturn the historical and systematic conception of the self by suggesting that it has an autonomous life. This development of subjectivity into its own space is very much like the epiphany of language, especially when Kierkegaard asserts its novel independence from permanent or exterior 'truth' in his *Journal* of August 1, 1835: "The thing is to find a truth which is true for me, to find the idea for which I can live and die."

In answer to Nietzsche's insistent question, who is it that is speaking, Kierkegaard answers "the existing human being . . . the concrete empirical being. Only with the concrete does becoming enter in, and it is from the concrete that abstract thought abstracts." This emphasis on what is "concrete" will emerge again in another context, and it will be revealing to note its origin here in the deconstruction of all systematic truths and values—which will include, of course, the reified Man of humanism. Kierkegaard is the first to root certainty in individual existence, and in an idea of individual passion. The point is made in *Concluding Unscientific Postcript*, his manifesto of subjectivity: "Only such knowledge as has an essential relationship to existence is essential knowledge." This is Kierkegaard's version of Socratic dialectic, this continual return to the values of lived experience, to the lineaments of the individual man and to "the fact that the knower is an existing individual". The once self-certain truths of systematic thought become invaded by paradox, because they are now chosen as objective only in the passion and uncertainty of subjective life.

But this sense of individual truth is not one that is easily acquired; for Kierkegaard, it is the Christian therapeutic which succeeds despair. Its progress takes place in perpetual uncertainty, the uncertainty and ambiguity of 'becoming', and it represents a life very different from that of systematic philosophy. Since Kierkegaard places the selfhood in its own space, the life which it develops runs parallel to that of the growing autonomy of language. For Kierkegaard, the selfhood exists beyond language, whether it be Hegelian logocentrism or Mallarmé's strained discourse. The self is prior to language and its relations, and from this time the self and language diverge with such a momentum that they never again touch at any point.

But how, then, can Kierkegaard's written texts be described? His own description is helpful: "If I desired to communicate anything on this point, it would first of all be necessary to give my exposition an indirect form . . . the contrast of the form is the measure of inwardness." His style is maieutic and indirect; since there are no certain or objective truths to be transmitted, language loses its immediacy and its conventional plainness. Language no longer discloses 'being', since "more important than the truth is the manner in which truth is accepted". It can only be received amid all the individuality and discontinuity of the self, and Kierkegaard's own writing comes very close to Nietzsche's sense of the varieties of interpretation that overlay any original 'text'. He deploys a number of pseudonyms, for example, to cloak the authorship of his works with a dramatic and multiple significance, and there is an indirection and concealment of meaning within the particular contours of the individual voice. And it is in this context that Kierkegaard draws strength from the movement of modernism, in his direct resistance to the self-identity and transparency of orthodox discourse. His affirmation of individual existence overturns those humane 'values' which the language once embodied. To call his work 'existentialist' is to beg the question, and all that need be described here is the presence of a thought that reinterprets the selfhood as fundamentally as literature reinterprets language. The self becomes a new thing: it is this self which is substantiated in the enquiries of Husserl and Heidegger, and which is excluded from our own culture which maintained (and still maintains) the conventional and systematic version of subjectivity.

Of course the writings of Edmund Husserl and his pupil, Martin Heidegger, have been variously interpreted and analysed but, at the risk of imposing a false unity upon two very complex sets of description, it may be revealing to see their work upon the common ground of modernism. The central development in Husserl's analysis lies in his formalising of that concept of concrete "experience" which Kierkegaard had first disclosed. Husserl initiates "eidetic phenomenology", or what can be called the science of appearances, since he takes as his model of obvious fact the carnal presence of things in the world. Husserl places Kierkegaard's sense of subjectivity as experience upon a transcendental ground; this may seem paradoxical and perhaps retrogressive, but in *Ideen* Husserl's departure from any rational metaphysic or aesthetic is made clear: "Eidetic phenomenology is the realm of essential structures of transcendental subjectivity immediately transparent to the mind . . . being entirely intuitive it proves refractory to every methodically devised scheme of constructive symbolism." Our experience is not implicated in a permanent state or truth of being for "the life of the soul is made intelligible in its most intimate and intuitional essence, and this original intuitional essence lies in a constitution of meaning-formations in modes of existential validity which is perpetually new and incessantly organising itself afresh". "Meaning" does not reside in a rational construction or human truth but in the specific, individual processes of intention.

Self-investigation on the Husserlian model is not a quest for self-certainty, but one that can only be continued within the context of existence. *Cartesian Investigations* returns to this theme: "We have trusted transcendental experience [of the ego] because of its originarily lived-through experience." It is this concept of transcendental experience which Husserl is the first to recognise— it is not the "experience" of the humanist, to be transformed into moral or aesthetic forms, but the concrete ground of an absolute ontology. But how can experience be translated into absolute terms? Husserl returns to what he sees as the origins of knowledge, in the transcendental act of consciousness. It is a consciousness of "essences". But these essences do not exist beyond appearance or experience, as they do in conventional epistemology, they exist within them: "only in appearances stripped of all that is foreign to them can essences legitimately be found." It is a new world of things that can now be recognised, and no longer the divided world of metaphysics searching for meaning. This act of "stripping", of recognising the essence, is the work of the subjective consciousness which grasps the appearance by its "intention toward it". For Husserl, the essence of whatever is is contained in the subjective act whereby it is brought to consciousness. And it is this absolute inter-relation between subject and the world of appearances which prompts one of Husserl's most incisive remarks, in *Crisis of European Man*: "In so far as the intuitive environing world, purely subjective as it is, is forgotten in the scientific thematic, the working subject is also forgotten, and the scientist is not studied." The fruit of this insight appears, of course, in the work of Heisenberg and Böhr.

And so Husserl's transcendental ego transcends the split between a Cartesian subjectivity and the scientific 'objectivity' which is its natural twin. The intentionality of experience postulates the existence of the object on the same terms as that of the subject, since "a concrete description of the sphere of consciousness as a self-contained sphere of intentionality also calls, of necessity, for a description of the object as such, referred to in intentional experience and its objective meaning". And just as "the ego constitutes in himself something 'other', something Objective", so we may assume our own experience only in the recognition of "fellow-subjects" as "co-transcendental". They constitute the "lebenswelt", the lived world, which Husserl came to emphasise more and more frequently as the ground of his investigations.

Husserl's concept of the self, then, is quite distinct from that of a rationalist metaphysic and that of humanism. In its grasping of appearances, it is the act itself which is vital: this entry of experience and of the 'other' as constituting the ego. The order of the selfhood is not an aesthetic or an anthropological one, but is rather constituted by pre-predicative experience: an experience that exists prior to language and its imposition of a network of syntactical relations. "Self" and "non-self", "inner" and "outer", "essence" and "existence" are transcended as categories by a conception of primary experience. The aesthetic bond between self and language, giving unity to one and value to the other, is finally untied.

The writings of Martin Heidegger take advantage of this freer life, but they do so in a spirit very different from that of Husserl; Heidegger invokes an apparently ancient spirit, and resumes the question of Being. This might seem very much a rear-guard action, especially after Kierkegaard's polemic against systematic or permanent truths. But Heidegger does not dwell within the space of a conventional metaphysic, and his texts carry over the themes of that modernism which we have been elucidating. In *What is Metaphysics?*, his words echo those of Kierkegaard: "Metaphysical questioning has always to be based on the essential situation of existence, which puts the question." And that which is rooted in existence, which puts the question, is for Heidegger "Dasein" or "There-being". It becomes the grand theme of *Sein und Zeit*: "This entity which each of us is himself and which includes enquiry as one of its possibilities of being, we shall denote by the term *Dasein*." The development of *Sein und Zeit* treats of this horizon of man's existence, grounded as it is in temporality.

How are we to speak of *Dasein*? There is no point in entering the warm circle of Heidegger's hermeneutic, much opaque commentary has already traced that path, and all that can be done here is to suggest the family of his concerns. *Dasein* is not subjective, since it manifests itself in the beings that surround us; it is not concealed as an "essence" or inner cause since it lies in the act of existence itself. Heidegger evokes at this point a phenomenology which will be ". . . a science of the Being of entities . . . grasping its objects in such a way that everything about them which is up for discussion must be treated by exhibiting it directly and demonstrating it directly." The ground is that of the experienced world which does not conceal its meanings, and we have to abandon that metaphysical quest for what lies "behind" appearances: ". . . thinking did not reach its goal by using the language of metaphysics."

It is with this sense of the lived world unveiling its meanings that Heidegger is able to transcend the dichotomy of subject and object. *Dasein* is within the two: it is prior to the emergence of any external relation, and actually renders its presence possible. The selfhood is not a self-contained entity, but exists within *Dasein* in the consciousness of Being: "*Dasein* in itself is essentially being-with . . . being-with is an existential characteristic of *Dasein* even when factically no Other is present-at-hand or perceived." Experience and the experiencing subject are at the centre of his enquiry: but it is not a determined and determinate space, this experience, it is rather a continually ambiguous ground. *Dasein* exists within what-is-in-totality, which is necessarily indeterminate in our local, actual existence and borders vaguely around "what-is". This concept of "what-is-in-totality" is not one to be easily analysed, and it is necessary to proceed by indirection to the centre of Heidegger's design.

There is, first, Heidegger's conception of the necessity of "untruth" within the world, an idea whose origin can be located in the writings of Nietzsche. In *Hölderlin and The Essence of Poetry*, Heidegger develops this theme in connection with *Dasein* since "Dissimulation is the ground phenomenon of *Dasein*. For Man clings to the selfhood and whatever is accessible." This grasping of whatever is closest to hand, this fixing of names and meanings lets what-is-in-totality, the horizon of experience, slip away. "For when something is revealed in itself, the what-is-in-totality is concealed (is untruth)." In this sense, all of those 'meanings' to which we cling as certainties can only be established upon the basis of a larger untruth, and it is within this non-meaning that we locate ourselves: "This concealment, or authentic untruth, is anterior to all revelation of this or that reality . . . it is the authentic dis-essence of truth." And this is the universe which Nietzsche had first disclosed in *Beyond Good and Evil*: "We must admit untruth as a necessary condition of life." The apparent being of objects is part of a greater concealment, and the values to which we accede are invaded with non-meaning. This was, of course, the pressure which overturned seventeenth-century modernism and which was prominent in the texts of De Sade; Heidegger maintains the pressure in his own investigation into "Nothing".

We have come across "Nothing" before: it marked the demise of classical rationalism, and the troubling birth of literature in the

70

work of Flaubert and De Sade, but it is Heidegger who first lays the ambiguous force open for enquiry. The emphasis on Being leads directly to the question of Non-Being: "Nothing is at one with what-is-in-totality." This is from *What is Metaphysics?* which attempts to answer the question, how can Nothing be recognised? The answer may be a familiar one at this late date, since it derives from a mood which has already been located elswhere: "Dread reveals Nothing." This is very like Kierkegaard's sense of dread as that in which the selfhood finds itself when it is deprived of objective truths; it was dread, too, which marked the rise of literature since it is dread that feeds off the fact that something —whether it be the self or whether it be written language—is, literally, 'about' nothing. It reveals the boundaries of what exists: "Nothing is that which makes the revelation of what-is as such possible for human existence. Nothing not merely provides the conceptual opposite of what-is, but it is also an original part of essence." It is that principle which throws us into Being and which is the horizon of our experience. "Man's *Dasein* can only relate to what-is by projecting into Nothing. Going beyond what-is is of the essence of *Dasein*." That principle, which is also that movement of life which initiated the modern movement in Europe, becomes here the centre of philosophical enquiry; the positive dispensation of classical rationalism, and that transparent language of truths through which it is evoked, are finally displaced in the opaque and involuted language of Heidegger.

The theme of language and of its new dispensation is also one on which Heidegger expands. His awareness of the autonomy of language is the central focus of his investigations, since language "consists in the origination of Being through words . . . it is the House of Being . . . naming discloses the Being of beings". In his overturning of classical metaphysics, he also overturns the humanism which it had developed: "Language is not a tool at Man's disposal, rather it is that event which disposes of the supreme possibility of human existence." This is the context for his essays on Hölderlin, Anaximander and Träkl, and the theme develops into a general interrogation of Being. The foundation of human existence rests in language, which is the "hailing" of Being. Heidegger describes what he sees as the fundamental word, the utterance of

71

Being, and since he works within a concept of the *spoken* language he does not concern himself with the self-certainty and presence-to-itself of the written language. For Heidegger, language is the pure presence of Being of which temporal human existence is a part. But Being is mediated through Nothing; the spoken Language both originates in Man, and yet denies his local being—his 'meaning'.

Then what is Man? Heidegger denies that the selfhood has any identity or stability: ". . . we need to leave behind the achievements of subjectivity," and he asks, in *Letter on Humanism*, "Who is it, then, who has taken over Being as everyday Being-with-one another?" (This closely resembles Nietzsche's question, Who is it that is speaking?) Heidegger's answer is that "the 'who' is not this or that one, not oneself, not some people, and not the sum of them all. The who is the neuter, the 'they' (Das Man)". Humanism is the "absolute objectivisation of everything" since it presupposes the essence of man and interprets the whole world from this fixed perspective. Humanism may even resurrect the image of man in the aesthetic appreciation of art, "but the more isolatedly the work stands in itself, and the more purely it seems to dissolve all connections with human beings, the more simply does the thrust, that such a work *is*, move into the open" (from *The Origin of the Work of Art*). Being is not the prerogative of man, since it is grounded within the incarnate world of existence. The experience of man does not rest upon any permanent truth, but within the horizon of untruth and the nothingness which discloses being. It is within these formulations that the development of the modern movement can be traced. Kierkegaard, Husserl and Heidegger establish a phenomenology which has nothing whatever to do with the internal relations of language, but it is one that works just as surely to displace the values of humanism and a rationalist aesthetic.

And at this time of transition, at the time of the writings of Husserl and Heidegger, were there any developments in our own culture: were there, in other words, any heirs to the modernism of Joyce and Eliot? There seem not to have been, and what persisted was that old dualism of subject and object which Eliot and Joyce had been struggling to transform. But their work was not recognised on these terms; Pound's *Draft of XXX Cantos* and

Auden's *Poems* were both published in 1930, and it was the direction of these two texts that was to dominate written poetry into our own time. They found successors because they placed themselves firmly within the old tradition—the tradition which still enmeshes our national perception.

The form and appearance of the *Cantos* might seem to deny this, since what is there except a surfeit of modernity? It holds together many texts: letters, myth, anecdote, economic speculation and impassioned polemic. There is even some Chinese calligraphy. The reader enters a diverse world of visual, rather than aural, connotation. Different forms of language and dialect, diverse areas of time, are located together and preserved within a sacrosanct writing:

> To know the histories
>
> to know good from evil
> And know whom to trust.
>
> Ching Hao.
> Chi crescera
> (Paradiso)
> "of societies" said Emmanuel Swedenborg
> Mr Jefferson lining up for Louis Philippe,
> a fact which should have been known to
> M. de Tocqueville.

The expansive design here, placed within a loosened syntax, breaks away from the formality of Pound's earlier poetry and employs space in ways similar to that, for example, of Mallarmé's *Un Coup de Dés*. The design is a purely written one, since the disparate areas of language are not reconciled by anything like a "voice" of Pound. The poem has no aural base since there is no 'subject' speaking through it: so it is that all styles exist on similar terms, and there are no 'high' or 'low' types of language. Pound retreats from the subjective sphere by means of this gesture, since the idea of what is 'poetic' and what is 'unpoetic' is a simple strategy of the divided self, trying to find residence in a protected manner of delivery. Pound deconstructs this sense of a poetic writing.

But to say that Pound, like Joyce, excises the privileged consciousness of the subject from the *Cantos* is not to say that he creates a literature as Joyce did. Speech, in his earlier poetry, is given a formal objectivity by allusion and reference; in the *Cantos* there is a different kind of factuality and referentiality at its centre —it takes its form from its polemical intent. It is not a literature because it clings to the certainty of its rhetoric and to the truth-giving power of its language:

> To John's bro, the sheriff, we lay a kind word in passing
> > Cromwell was not prudent
> > > nor honest
> > > > nor laudable
>
> Prayer: hands uplifted
> Solitude: a person, a NURSE. . . .
>
> whereof 4 crops a year, seed he had of Gridley of Abingdon
> pods an odd thing, a sort of ramshorn of straw. . . .
>
> Light & the flowing crystal,
> > never gin in cut glass had such clarity. . . .

There is a sparseness and hardness about the writing; the direct movement of the line, the fullness of the language on the denotative surface, hold the meaning forward; the experience of meaning is conveyed, without a theme actually appearing. The *Cantos* have a content but not a subject—or, rather, its subject is its own argument since the many texts have a source outside themselves and are included only as rhetorical *exempla*. Critics come up against this fact of their external origin by postulating an external order that would unite the poem: otherwise, it seems to them, the objectivity would be fragmented and uncertain. I would rather say that we experience an unattached objectivity for its own sake, and that the *Cantos* embody the pure movement of meaning without reference. But 'objectivity' can only be a metaphor for the self-sufficiency of language, since the ambiguity of a literature rests precisely on its transcending 'objectivity' as well as 'subjectivity'. But the *Cantos* are grasped by a certainty that can only look outwards, and all its power is realised on its exterior, in its encycopaedic and technical assurance. It has, in fact, a false objectivity, and it is this false objectivity which has shaped much recent poetry —William Carlos Williams's *Paterson* and Charles Olson's *Maximus* sequence, for example, derive from Pound's earlier texts. All of these writings are eager to discard the tenuous selfhood, but they do so in terms of a naïve dualism and their work becomes 'objective', established upon a sense of place or local history. They use the written language without recognising its actual powers, and its ability to transcend the object as well as the subject.

Only Auden has an instinctive grasp of these powers. He, like Pound, is entranced by the truth-giving, and in his case the diagnostic and abstracting, powers of language (in this sense his is a rhetoric rather than a poetry), but Auden also recognises this manœuvre for what it is. He does not use the truth-giving powers of language blindly but plays with them formalistically and places them at the centre of a larger design. I could put the same point another way by noting that he exploits with mastery the possibilities of English poetry as they have existed in their conventional form. To be conventional is not, of course, to be reactionary. When we discuss the voice of his poetry we are dealing with the most traditional and persistent quality of English poetry, but one that in his work gains a new strength and subtlety of emphasis:

> Consider this and in our time
> As the hawk sees it or the helmeted airman

or

> Faces along the bar
> Cling to their average day.

The strength of line in those passages, within its assured rhythm and diction, derives from an individual voice but one which, by virtue of its individual presence, can assimilate what are normally irreconcilable areas of language. The language of the *Cantos* is pre-eminently a written one, and so it tended toward fragmentation, but in the poetry of Auden it is spoken, and so can combine variation by means of the fullness of its origin. Here is a passage from Auden's *Matthew Arnold*:

> His gift knew what he was—a dark, disordered city,
> Doubt hid it from the father's fond chastising cry
> Where once the mother-forms had glowed protectively
> Stood the haphazard alleys of the neighbour's pity . . .

This is not an enduring poetry because the principles of Auden's manner become too apparent. Adjective and noun, verb and adverb are yoked together by the formality of the poem, so that objects and scenes can be presented in a language of ethical judgement ("disordered city . . . glow protectively . . . haphazard alleys") while private feelings and responses are given a detached and neutral air. It is the same tone which creates

> Lay your sleeping head, my love,
> Human, on my faithless arm

and which establishes a dispassionate, if not analytic, poise above passion. There is no uncertainty about this voice. Subjective feeling and objective judgement are grounded within a synthetic medium of expression, an expression that gains its stability from Auden's brilliant deployment of poetic form. But this synthesis between subject and object is one that remains external (like Auden's theoretical attempts at synthesis, first in Marxism and then in a version of Christian humanism); because the voice relies upon a formal order, it suffers from a certain deficiency.

But it is a deficiency that Auden is able to turn into a part of his theme, and the irresolution of subject and object within the self-certainty of his medium becomes his poetic context. This has sometimes been described in terms of external opposition and paradox:

> Desire like a police dog is unfastened. . . .

The tension of the poetic self, that is assumed, with the world of recalcitrant objects and ethical abstractions, is maintained by Auden's continual shifting from 'concrete' to 'abstract', specific to general. Sometimes this has an allegorical flavour:

> Scandal with her sharp knees up. . . .

although the physical here does not interpenetrate with the abstract; they exist beside each other in explicit commentary:

> it is time for the destruction of error
> The chairs are being brought in from the garden . . .

and it is this disjunction which evokes the humour of Auden's poetry, that raffish tone between schoolboy and schoolmaster.

76

Auden's is not a literature, it is a rhetoric. It enlarges and strengthens Anglo-Saxon forms, but it does not change the expression of them: there is still that same poetic self and the same objectivity which goes beside it. Auden retains conventional lyric and narrative forms while changing their immediate content. His is a poetry of direct statement, in which he employs a generalised diction:

> Harrow the house of the dead; look shining at
> New styles of architecture, a change of heart

but he places this diction within a lyric context that, with a rhythmic and harmonic accompaniment, can elicit a sensory response. In retaining a poetic voice, Auden must also retain the aesthetic category which exists in a certain tension with his generalised and objective statements. This is his significance in the development of our culture: that he can retain the aesthetic potential of his voice while appearing to abandon a private and subjective content. He develops a language that still exists within the relation of subject and object, but one that because of its tonal certainty offers gratification to the troubled self.

If Auden became the central figure of his time because of his resolution of the possibilities of English poetry, so F. R. Leavis became its most significant critic, because of his conviction of the strength of a specifically English 'tradition'. His unique responsiveness, and his persistent failure, derive from this evocation of an English 'literature'. Leavis's writings have redefined academic notions of 'poetry' and 'tradition', as they appear to us in a national guise. His critical works have exercised a pervasive influence in the teaching of literature in the universities and schools and if the contemporary loss of confidence in literary studies within these institutions is to be understood, it is first necessary to understand the contribution which Leavis made to the study of English.

New Bearings in English Poetry was published in 1932, and although its effect was not immediate, it came to significantly alter critical awareness. It was the first intelligent response to the poetry of Eliot and of Pound, and the first attempt to reinvigorate the criticism of the period. It is not that the criticism of Leavis is wholly original, it was not designed to be so. He is by critical temperament less inclined to the kind of general and theoretical enquiry which overturns orthodox critical categories, and he prefers to recognise instead what is actual and specific in the language of poetry. It is within this emphasis, an emphasis which is as strong in Quiller-Couch as it is in Leavis, that we will come across critical precepts which have been discovered elsewhere in this study.

The description of *New Bearings* can start at any point. For Leavis, the power of the poet lies in "a capacity for experiencing and a power of communicating" and, since it bears the brunt of Leavis's assertiveness, we may ask—the experiencing of what? "The poet has the power of making words express what he feels . . . poetry can communicate an actual quality of experience": and it was this version of "experience" which has been employed earlier, in the critical essays of Eliot. Language is seen, typically, as an instrument to communicate a certain range or quality of this experience, although the concept of experience as such is never analysed and remains merely as a moral imperative. In this sense it can be contrasted with that novel idea of experience which the German phenomenologists were developing, in their attempt to redefine the nature of the involvement of the person in the world. Leavis's construct of 'experience' owes more to a traditional sense of the moral self and its claims: it simply remains as that area which embodies truth.

But this emphasis is not, of course, unique to Leavis and it serves little purpose to fault him for not appreciating the theoretical context of his claims for poetry. What has, rather, come to seem characteristically his own is his ethical stance. He generally adopts the tone of the moralist: "vulgar" and "cheap" become familiar epithets and Browning, for example, is described as "possessing an inferior mind and spirit". But what is Leavis's touchstone of value? Since he has established what he calls "concrete experience" as an aesthetic phenomenon, it is not surprising that he derives his standards from within its sphere; the qualities which he admires in the work of Eliot and Pound, for example, are those of "subtlety, flexibility and complexity", where a mode of experience becomes a way of describing language.

Where the German phenomenologists had redefined 'experience' so that it diverges widely from the formal relations of language, Leavis considers those relations as existing within the same context, the context of moral truth, as those of experience.

That triad of affective qualities—subtlety, flexibility and complexity—marks Leavis's permanent stand in matters of critical judgement. His readings derive from it, and its significance is everywhere taken for granted. But these qualities do indeed have a particular context and a particular origin, although they generally remain hidden from view. Where, for example, does Leavis's sense of "concrete experience" emerge but from Kierkegaard's sense of the "concrete empirical being" as the ground of all truth? It could be said that Kierkegaard's notion of the "aesthetic man", dwelling within his passions, is analogous to Leavis's own critical position. But this resemblance cannot be pressed too far, since Leavis's sense of the individual response that lies beyond systematic theory is couched in very different terms from that of Kierkegaard. For Kierkegaard, it is the perilous and problematic conclusion of a Christian therapeutic, where for Leavis it is the assumed and permanent ground of his whole enquiry.

And it becomes an inevitable part of Leavis's aesthetics of experience that his criticism should embody a theory of the poetic 'selfhood'. He discusses *The Waste Land* in a perspective which is certainly partial and may well be contradictory: ". . . it is an effort to focus upon an inclusive human consciousness." There is a consistent concern in his critical texts with poetic "sensibility" and with the integrity of the poet's "emotions". But this is in a period when the selfhood is in most doubt: even Kierkegaard's subjective truth is rooted in paradox and certain change. Leavis seems to be unaware of the difficulties which crowd within his critical focus, although he goes so far as to underline the instability of his idea of "inclusive human consciousness" by emphasising its ambiguities. He describes the poet as "the co-presence in the mind of a number of different orientations, fundamental attitudes and orders of experience". He converts what might otherwise be seen as definite symptoms of decline (if we are concerned, that is, with an *integral* self) into the criteria of aesthetic and experiential worth. The instability of the self in derived from the sudden access of moral experience: it is a strange dualism, and where does 'literature' impinge upon it?

Leavis's *Revaluations*, published in 1936, mark the point of Leavis's maximum impact upon the academic community; he formulates what is still considered to be the viable tradition of English poetry, and he does so on exactly those terms which are established in *New Bearings*. The book is an extension of the first criticism, and it is in fact part of a larger unity: in the sense that Leavis's idea of tradition differs very little from that of Eliot. It is for Leavis "a kind of ideal and impersonal living memory" and, like Eliot, he introduces an unexplained alchemy in his notion of the emotive and specific constituents of that ideal order. It is the alchemy of a traditional humanism.

There are emphases in *Revaluations*, in fact, which make it less of an original than its title suggests. I could put the point differently by noting that the poets and the poems which Leavis praises may be different from those praised by Quiller-Couch, but the context is the same. Leavis's demotion of Milton is an example: he says of Miltonic discourse that "it has no particular expressive worth". But of what might this "expression" consist? Leavis describes it in an analysis of a particularly 'good' passage of Milton: "The total effect is as if words withdrew themselves from the focus of our attention, and we were directly aware of a tissue of feelings and perceptions." This becomes Leavis's central claim, that words exist as the transparencies through which 'feelings' shine, and that the poem offers us the texture of a language only in order to elicit a response to those "feelings". We are to recognise the moral and human pattern behind the poem, and we are to see the poem in the light of our humane experience.

This has, of course, been the horizon of Anglo-Saxon critical theory throughout the period of this analysis, since it is rooted in an orthodoxy which has persisted despite the momentum of modernism in Europe. Leavis's constant evaluation is in terms of a concrete and passionate individuality. Ben Jonson has "a talking voice . . . a mimetic flexibility of language"; the highest form of poetic language is the "speech that belongs to the emotional and sensory texture of actual living". And it is Leavis's predilection for an idea of 'speech' that is emphasised in his concern for individual 'presence' within the poem. In *Revaluations* Wordsworth is described as having "an immediate personal urgency", Shelley has "a weak grasp upon the actual" and Keats "a wilful delimitation of the 'true' and 'real' in experience". This is not in fact specific or 'practical' criticism, it is a criticism that rests quite comfortably within a moral orthodoxy. It relies upon an aesthetic in which it is experience that offers what is personal and true, real and actual. Its space is one in which self and language interpenetrate to form a rhetoric of meaning. Leavis has an urgency and a moral fervour which is able to reclaim the finest spirit of this literary humanism, but his fervour serves to confirm, too, the pressures under which it was legitimately giving way.

But Anglo-Saxon criticism does not, of course, spring fully armed from the writings of Dr Leavis; during the late 'thirties and early 'forties a more abstract and descriptive critical language became popularised in the writings of John Crowe Ransom and Cleanth Brooks. It became known as the "new criticism", although any activity which declares itself as "new" requires careful study since self-conscious novelty is the most traditional of strategies. In this instance, Cleanth Brooks's *The Well-Wrought Urn* is one of the central studies, and it had a formative effect upon criticism in both England and America.

The criticism which the book offers is one that describes itself as "new" because it is established upon a highly formalistic interpretation of the poem—now considered, for this purpose, as a self-sufficient 'unit' of language. Brooks's criticism apparently abandons Leavis's description of the perceptual and emotional simulacrum of the poem in order to concentrate upon what is called its internal structure of meaning. The psychological metaphors are in part replaced by logical and spatial metaphors, and the thrust of the analysis recedes from the perceiving subject to the structure of the object. The analysis can only be tentative here because, despite its formalistic pretensions, the "new criticism" is less incisive and less significant than, for example, the formalist work of the Russian and Bulgarian Schools. Writers like Zirminsky and Tyrjanov construct it as an encompassing discipline, as a study of what is seen as a literary system of functions which can be recorded and verified. Theirs is a strict formalism which is still

81

NOTES FOR A NEW CULTURE

operating in Paris and Prague while our own "new criticism" was only locally effective, and owed more to its immediate context than to any fundamental redirection of critical interests. It was certainly not "new" in any but a superficial and technical sense, since the structure which Brooks analyses in *The Well Wrought Urn* is primarily a conventional, affective one: "The structure meant is a structure of meanings, evaluations and interpretations, and the principle of unity which informs it seems to be one of balancing and harmonising connotations, attitudes, and meaning." When put like that, criticism enters that traditional sphere which we have recognised everywhere in Anglo-Saxon culture; the metaphors are those of individual psychology, and the emphasis rests upon a version of sensory harmony and rational lucidity. The 'structure' resides in the unity of the aesthetic effect of the poem, and not in the relation of its internal characteristics.

Brooks's conventional stance comes forward again in his description of poetry as "the language of paradox"; this is simply an assertion on a quasi-syntactical level of those qualities of complexity and subtlety which Leavis had formulated on a psychological level. Brooks describes the poet as "working by contradiction and qualification . . . his use of irony, paradox, ambiguity and complexity of attitudes". Here, as in Leavis, the problematic self is present as the ground of Brooks's enquiry—a self divided and expressing itself through paradox. There is certainly nothing like an adequately formalistic interpretation of the language of poetry, however we conceive of it, in Brooks's contention that "the structural unity of the poem lies in the unification of attitudes into a hierarchy subordinated to a total and governing attitude." The formalism here is one that appeals to an orthodox individualistic and sensory response, since it is one in which language is mediated through a human unity. The poem is still an "aesthetic structure" which "unifies experience", and Brooks returns to the earliest of rationalistic credos.

But Brooks's 'formalism' is designed to be prescriptive; the structuralist interpretation is offered as an alternative to critical relativism, and as a return to valid judgements of 'good' and 'bad' poetry. Brooks has attempted to combine aestheticism with a critical positivism—which is not as difficult an undertaking as it

82

sounds, since they share the same context. And that context is what Brooks calls "a defence of the humanities"; his formalistic metaphors are essentially part of that interregnum when humanism (under the guise of the 'humanities' or the 'human sciences') searches for adequate specific categories or for an adequate neo-positivism: adequate in the sense that they can be seen to be grounded in something other than subjective consciousness. But Brooks still treats the language of poetry as "expressive"— "poems are about man himself"—and so he cannot excise the claims of the subject from his 'objective' analysis. A scientific method only increases the force of the invisible human agent. Brooks has transposed Eliot's and Leavis's sense of individual consciousness, or sensibility, into another context. It is one of "common structural principles" and "a powerful structure of attitudes", so that the content and evaluation of this "structure" are essentially the same as those which reside within the sphere of aesthetic subjectivity. The "new criticism" provides a revised humanism, since it is one that is as fundamentally rationalistic and aesthetic as before.

This is the general context of Anglo-Saxon critical thought, and it is one that persists despite the attempts of German phenomenologists to relocate the selfhood in a world of lived experience. It is only in the work of the French 'existentialists', who were the contemporaries of those critics whose work we have just been describing, that we encounter any development of that new theme which the Germans had expounded. The two most prominent of these French philosophers, Sartre and Merleau-Ponty, affirm their debt to the first investigations of Husserl while at the same time pressing the direction of his thought in ways that now opened for the first time.

Sartre's most original text, *Being and Nothingness*, was published in 1943. Its debt to Husserlian method becomes apparent in Sartre's affirmation of the intentionality of consciousness and in his distinction between a "pre-reflective consciousness", which is the immediate and unmediated experience of ourselves in the world, and the "reflective consciousness", which is the sphere of the imagination and the understanding. But this is only the beginning of Sartre's analysis, and although it shares the same open field as phenomenology (or what Sartre calls in *Saint Genet* the search "to reconcile the subject and the object") Sartre develops his thought into an entirely different form, and in a context other than that of purely philosophical description.

Sartre emphasises the duality which is apparently trying to transcend, or at least to "reconcile", in his description of "the shattering appearance of the consciousness of our own selfhood" and its "freedom", and conversely in his description of "the object" and the viscosity and self-subsistence of "things". It is in the spirit of this last formula that existentialism has been described as "a return to things themselves". This was, of course, precisely the aim of the English empiricists, more than two centuries before, and it is in this spirit, too, that Sartre returns to a Cartesian space in his concept of a subjective consciousness which, although it presumes the existence of the 'Other', is described as a monad existing in a state of privation: "My original fall is the existence of the Other." Sartre fundamentally redefines Husserlian intentionality by distinguishing between the intentional movement and the reflexive aspiration of consciousness: "consciousness of something" is not merely the letting-appear of the object, it is also the aspiration to become that object. Sartre describes the self as a "hole in the midst of Being"; consciousness is condemned not only to its own freedom, but to the project of being absolute, of being a subject and yet attaining to the status of the object which appears before it. But this "being-in-itself as well as being-for-itself" is an impossible condition; it is contradictory and it fails: "Man is a useless passion." This rather generalised anthropology is very different from Husserl's careful enquiry into the self, and its facile pessimism explains something of the narrowness and restrictiveness of Sartre's concept of subjectivity. Despite Sartre's obeisance to the earlier writings of phenomenology, his own work is firmly established upon that dichotomy of subject and object which had been overturned in the process of Husserlian intentionality and in Husserl's concept of *lebenswelt*, or the lived world. The horizon of Sartre's texts is an orthodox Cartesian one, with their sense of *res cogitans* (subject) and *res extensa* (things). For Sartre, the subject stands out before a recalcitrant material reality as either victim or conqueror.

The point has to be made like that in order to evoke something of the active and dramatic quality of Sartre's writings. He has said that "today, I think that philosophy is dramatic", and in fact *Being and Nothingness* was published five years after Sartre's novel, *La Nausée*, and at a time when Sartre was enjoying great literary success. His tendency within his philosophical writings, in fact, is to construe content and method in terms that are derived from rhetorical and literary discourse: literary methods outside literature are, of course, necessarily rhetorical. There are a great many concrete *exempla* and there is a great deal of descriptive narrative in *Being and Nothingness*, and theoretical matters are dramatised in texts like *Les Mouches*. Sartre's existentialism is, in this sense, a popular and utilitarian version of phenomenology. Moral and human truths are somehow extracted from phenomenological writings, and it is this acquiescence in a certain kind of public and social purpose that pushes Sartre's analysis toward more orthodox structures of meaning.

It is not surprising, then, that Sartre's attempt to utilise phenomenological explanation should lead him to espouse a form of humanism, despite the efforts of Husserl and Heidegger to overturn the formulae of humanism. And Sartre's *Existentialism and Humanism* discloses the extent of this reversal, although it is one that has been anticipated throughout this analysis. For Sartre's humanism becomes part of an insistence that experience is primarily a subjective phenomenon, based upon a Cartesian consciousness: "At the point of departure there cannot be any other truth than this, I think, therefore I am, which is the absolute truth of consciousness as it appears to itself . . . this theory alone is compatible with the dignity of Man, it is the only one which does not make man into an object." Here is a notion of Man which derives from the pure movement of subjectivity, and it is that 'Man' which has already appeared in other contexts. But Sartre differentiates his own notion from that of a conventional humanism; this last began with the proposition about human nature which, according to Sartre, "upholds Man as the supreme value". But it is difficult to see how Sartre's own humanism does anything other than change its terms: "Man is free, Man is freedom . . . he is himself the heart and centre of transcendence. There is no other

85

universe except the human universe and the universe of human subjectivity." Sartre creates an anthropology which departs from Husserl's foundation in an unmediated, concrete consciousness and which returns to the more familiar world of human attributes and individual existence.

Existence had first been described by Sartre as the concrete behaviour of intentional consciousness, but in his work it declines into a version of social positivism: Sartre commits himself to a popular humanism and a Marxism, although such commitment to objective system had once been described by Sartre as "inauthentic existence". It seems that, for Sartre, the only way to project my selfhood out of the narrow sphere of subjectivity is by an attachment to a meaning which sees "me" as one amongst many, as "the people" or as "Man". But this is no resolution of the crisis of subjectivity. Both individualism and humanism assuage the weary with a heightened sense of themselves, but theirs is essentially a rhetoric of private feeling.

The lines of this analysis can be gathered up at this point, in a recognition of the aesthetic fallacy within Sartre's humanism. It has been my continual claim that aesthetics and humanism are part of the same family of concepts, and so it is predictable that Sartre's aesthetic theory should, in certain crucial areas, be retrogressive. He parts company even with Kant's transcendental aesthetic and goes further back, to Edmund Burke, in order to construct a social and utilitarian aesthetic. This is indispensable for his sense of 'literature' as necessarily engaged in the struggle of the social world: "The writer has chosen to reveal the world and particularly to reveal man to other men so that the latter may assume full responsibility before the object which has thus been laid bare" (from *What is Literature?*). Words are once again the transparent ciphers of human action, just as they had been at the time of the first modernism in the seventeenth century.

This is, of course, merely the thematic surface of Sartre's pervasive orthodoxy; what is fundamental to his aesthetic is his sense of the art-object as embodying and unifying the aspirations of subjectivity in its "density of being-in-itself and for-itself". Its ground is a humanism which seeks in the forms of art a promise and a simulacrum of human well-being. Sartre's statement is that "each painting, each book, is a recovery of the totality of being. Each of them presents this totality to the freedom of the spectator. For this is quite the final goal of art: to recover the world by giving it to be seen as it is, but as if it had its source in human freedom." It is this fabricated freedom which is the context of humanism, and the perennial illusion of aesthetics is given a permanent ground in Sartre's ontology. Art is a paradigm for Man. Whatever we may think of Sartre's political commitments, his is an orthodox alternative to the development of modernism. He emphasises the bond between aesthetics and humanism, and their standing on a common ground of subjectivity.

Sartre's theme is a mosaic of many concerns, and we have seen that one of his strategies has been the interpenetration of "philosophy" with "literary" narrative—but their union can only be a rhetorical one. And it is in the writings of Merleau-Ponty that a strictly philosophical description of the self and of experience is continued. His primary text, the *Phenomenology of Perception*, was published two years after *Being and Nothingness*, and his reputation has been partly overshadowed by Sartre's activism. Merleau-Ponty is considered to be more 'academic', and this is his significant role since it describes very well his continuing effort to revalue conventional assumptions and to investigate their source and their context. This is a work that becomes essential when philosophies become slogans, and mediocrity a virtuous populism.

Specifically, Merleau-Ponty returns to a Husserlian analysis and repudiates Sartre's spurious dialectic between self and Other as "tronquée". Merleau-Ponty reasserts his intention to re-unite "subjective" and "objective" by proving them empty, in an appeal to *lebenswelt*, the world in which we actually find ourselves. It is that which is close at hand, and which Merleau-Ponty calls the "primary phenomenon". This is the centre of his work, this sense of the world which is to be revealed in the act of "eidetic reduction" which Husserl had formulated and which Merleau-Ponty now extends: "I attempt to reveal and make explicit in me the pure source of all the meanings which constitute the world around me and my empirical self." But this revelation is not to be constituted within a system, but in the realm of experience, in an investigation of the relations of the body to the world in primary consciousness. By "primary" is meant one in which perception exists before reflection; it is a world in which the first union is instinctive and habitual to ourselves: "It is the body that points out and speaks." Philosophy becomes rooted in our finite situation in the world, and no longer tries to constitute an absolute project. Its new situation is one that is described by Merleau-Ponty as "the consciousness of rationality in contingency" and what emerges in this description is that open space which Kierkegaard had recognised as "existence". The emergence of language into a formal unity has already been described in this analysis, and now an adjacent theme comes into prominence: it is the attempt of philosophy to locate the selfhood and its experience in something other than a rationalistic or humanistic system. It is this which Merleau-Ponty tries to develop in his philosophical writings.

His essay, *What is Phenomenology?* establishes the central claim: "In the silence of primary consciousness can be seen appearing not only what words mean but also what things mean: the core of primary meaning around which the acts of naming and expression take place. . . ." This silence, which is for Merleau-Ponty the origin of language, is that act of intention toward things and the world which is incarnate to us and this philosophy immediately becomes distinguished from the logocentrism of systematic thought: "Seeking the essence of consciousness will not mean escaping from existence into the universe of things said," and the world is no longer the humanist's one of 'meanings': ". . . looking for the world's essence is not looking for what it is as an idea once it has been reduced to a theme of discourse . . . the world is not what I think but what I live through." What is in operation here is the deconstruction of the rationalism and the humanism of the first modernism. It is the culmination of Husserl's *lebenswelt*, in which the concept of experience is not to be derived from pure subjectivity or from systematic and grammatical perceptions, but rather from a mode of being in the world and being with others: "Man is within the world; it is in the world that he recognises himself."

For Merleau-Ponty, the selfhood is not an ego but a state of attentiveness. It is a zone of possibilities into which we enter as we exist in our bodies. In *Phenomenology of Perception* it is stated that "The world is all in us, and I am all outside myself". Our relationship to the world is one of the mute expression of our gestures. But what, then, is the status of language? It dwells within the *speaking* subject, on the far side of the autonomy and self-sufficiency of written language. As far as Merleau-Ponty is concerned, speech is a mode of discovering ourselves within our own expressions. It embodies reflective, as opposed to primary, consciousness. Just as our body assumes the world, so speech assumes a landscape of thought and reflection which is not visible to us. It "teaches our involvement in the pre-constituted world . . . it is in the actual practice of speaking that I learn to understand". What is it that we understand in our speech? First, our own presence as subject within this 'outering-forth' of ourselves; but our subjectivity is not a self-contained phenomenon: "Subject is not a self-transparent thought absolutely present to itself." Language is an 'inter-subjective' phenomenon; it does not contain or transmit individual "meanings" but "supposes in the listener a creative re-enactment of what is heard". Language is not implicated in the expression of "truths", but in the open and successive community of experience: ". . . signification arouses speech as the world arouses my body—by a mute presence." Language is "expressive", not in the humanist sense of any meaning or any individual 'truth' which it embodies, but in the sense that it is rooted in a world which assumes the self without being interpreted or curtailed by it. It is as much the silent world as our private selves that speaks through language. This takes us a long way from Kierkegaard, but he is finally recalled here by this autonomous and open self, a self which—like language—has gone beyond the truths and ends of Man.

5

The Uses of Humanism

Love. Love. Love. All you need is love, love, love.
The Beatles.

(1) *Contrasts of the New*

This little history is now approaching that first moment in England
of formal self-consciousness; whether it be the "new novel" or the
"new drama", a writing appears which is described in terms of its
originality and which is identified as such. It became established in
certain works in the 'fifties, but I want first to describe two very
different works which were published during the last War and
which soon became acclimatised as 'representative' and 'modern'.
They are Eliot's *Four Quartets* and Joyce's *Finnegans Wake*—still
very close to our own time, closer in fact than anything which
has followed them, and within them may be hiding that inheritance of the 'new' which was later to be so vociferously taken up.

Joyce's *Ulysses* unfolds language in a comic transformation of
what was once fixed stylistically and called the 'real' world; it is
now within the power of the written language to create a world
out of itself, and Joyce returns to patristic sources in his evocation
of language, myth and human experience as parts of that opaque
λόγος which establishes the world. *Finnegans Wake* marks an increase in the strength of Joyce's attention to the insistent call of
language, the "messes of mottage" which are his theme. Puns,
parodies, nonsense-syllables, satire and alliteration merge with one
another in a continual harmony and life: "The untireties of lives-
living being the one substance of a streamsbecoming. Totalled in
toldteld and teldtold in tittletale tattle." But no single or 'speak-

90

ing' voice could master this telling. Mallarmé's affirmation concerned the fact that it is language which is speaking, but for Joyce it is not so much the language as the literary tradition which celebrates itself. He exercises with immense unreserve the resources of that historical consciousness which, in his work and in that of Eliot's, constitute our particular modernism. It becomes a living figure, on the verge of waking: "Be! Verb unprincipiant through the trancitive spaces." Everywhere Joyce evokes the discourse of other cultures: he employs nine or ten languages and Milton, Ibsen, the Koran, Augustine, Middle-English epic, Dickens, the Book of the Dead, and Byron are placed, not side by side, but within and among each other. He reinstates them within the endless opacity of his language without the benefit of their ostensible 'content'. There is no fixed perspective of meaning to unite the whole, since the contingency of that particular strategy has already been exposed: "A great primer must once for omniboss step rubrickredd out of the wordpress else there is no virtue more in alcohoran. For that (the rapt one warns) is what papyr is meed of, made of, hides and hints and misses of print. . . . So you need hardly spell me how every word will be bound over to carry three score and ten toptypsical readings throughout the book of Doublends Jined."

The language here creates a meaning, but not a sense. This is the paradox mediated by the activity of the language, with its continual verbal and tonal reminiscences which deconstruct a linear sense and replace it with the larger relationship of language to its own history. Its historical and technical range assure a continuity that does not depend upon 'action' or 'plot'; it is not implicated in the technical strategies of character and motive because no one discourse is fixed and successive. Everything exists in the continual present of the act of writing, and all possible meanings are contemporaneous. The complaint is often that *Finnegans Wake* is unreadable, and on one level that is perfectly true. We need not pay the usual ritual homage to Lewis Carroll to understand that nonsense is non-sense, and willingly so. Joyce frees language from a plainness of meaning, and from that notion of a "clear" style which is such a recent one in our history. He reinstates written techniques that have been lost to us since the seventeenth century, and the "common truth" of the plain style is overturned by the uncommon universe of discourse.

It is in this universe that Joyce works with the free association of harmony, rhythm and reference; language evokes language in the perpetual use of puns and analogies: "blank sheets in their faminy, my godfashioned bother near drave me roven maid," and a multiplicity of various meanings are delivered within this ravelled language. It would be as if the greatest wealth of experience were played out in the smallest possible space, were it not that the idea of 'experience' must be radically revised in the face of these words. It is not a private or traditional area of moral competence here, but one which derives solely from the autonomy and the arbitrariness of the written language. This language is the culmination of 'meaning' in the sense that it actually suggests everything, and it is a culmination, too, in the sense that meanings appear without the translucency of reference or denotation. It has been said that Joyce parodies the history of the world in *Finnegans Wake*, but this is the indispensable accompaniment to his foundation of a universal history of writing. His is the most expressive discourse of all.

This becomes clearer if its expressiveness is contrasted with that of Eliot in *Four Quartets*. This poem has been seen to embody a range of truths which works beyond the boundaries of 'literature', although the actual and living connection of Eliot and Joyce has already been described. Both writers are implicated in the unacknowledged progress of modernism, in their efforts to disperse and to deconstruct the selfhood in their language. In *Four Quartets*, just as surely as in *Finnegans Wake*, the self of moral experience is effaced and we are offered a "tradition" and "the words on the page". Eliot has been described as "the invisible poet", and this has indeed been the hallmark of modernism.

But there is little else to place *Four Quartets* within that space of literature which *Finnegans Wake* had opened. The poem is a meditation, and a communal one at that. It seems most accessible and it seems to approach our own most clear and substantial responses, and it is this accessibility—this legibility—which distinguishes it from Joyce's writing. The most familiar experience of the poem is of a sequence of voices, a succession of intimate and spoken thoughts which correspond to Eliot's sense of the "auditory imagination": "In writing verse I think that one is writing in terms of one's own voice: the way it sounds when you read it to yourself is the test."

But for Joyce, the word is pre-eminently written; it does not have the fullness of speech, and it needs to be elicited by sight and reading. It gains its potential and its glow of association from its appearance on the page, and it is primarily in this space that the historical lineaments of language can be disclosed. For Eliot, the word is spoken and comes out of the social and personal world of voices. Eliot wrote most of his verse drama before starting on *Four Quartets* (*The Cocktail Party*, for example, anticipates many of its themes) and he handles his poetry with that same dramatic and rhetorical potential. We hear different speakers, like the colloquial voice of the 'poet':

> So here I am in the middle way, having had twenty years,
> Twenty years largely wasted, the years of *l'entre deux guerres*. . . .

the voice of the loquacious preacher in 'Dry Salvages':

> I sometimes wonder if this is what Krishna meant—
> Among other things—or one way of putting the same thing. . . .

or the voice of objective lyrical statement:

> Garlic and sapphires in the mud
> Clot the bedded axle-tree. . . .

It is a dramatic poetry, but the language emerges from what becomes, finally, an impersonal voice. There is a dialectic of themes emerging through the sequence, in which one voice counterpoints another, to be reconciled in the final sequence of each quartet.

There is no opaqueness and no autonomy of language here, since *Four Quartets* is not a literature in the same sense as *Finnegans Wake*. The 'content' of the poem resides outside language and, although its theme is superficially a transcendental one, it is one that belongs within the area of human truths: to say that the poem is dramatic is to say that it is invaded by a kind of anthropocentrism. And it is this aesthetic humanism which Eliot confirms in his statement that the experience of the reader must be one of ". . . If I could write poetry, this is the way I would write it." Eliot's is a rhetoric which offers the reader a heightened version of his own concerns and of his own language: this is its intimacy. Joyce, on the other hand, offers us an epiphany of language without reference and nobody 'reads' *Finnegans Wake*. Eliot represents a meaning to which we can attach ourselves through that plain and vibrant speech:

> I can only say there we have been: but I cannot say where,
> And I cannot say, how long, for that is to place it in time. . . .

This goes 'beyond' poetry only in the sense that it offers a rhetoric of plain meaning, and not a literature.

Four Quartets is rhetorical, too, in its construction. It has a pervasive formality, in which different kinds of language are segregated and located in units which play against each other. Each quartet parallels *The Waste Land* with five sections, each with different metrical and harmonic patterns and each with a different 'voice'. In *Finnegans Wake* language spreads itself out into large areas, creating its own expansiveness as it extends from page to page. But for Eliot

> Only by the form, the pattern,
> Can words of music reach
> The stillness . . .

In *The Waste Land* Eliot tentatively evokes a language which emerged against his highly developed and almost classical sense of form. In *Four Quartets* Eliot experiments with form alone; he uses terza rima, iambic lyric patterns, long pentameters and narrative blank verse to achieve different kinds of meaning. And his dramatic voices are perhaps, in this context, the voices of form since it is the form that creates the meaning, and the dialectic of forms which arranges the dramatic life of the poetry.

There is indeed a 'meaning' within the poem, and it has been generally described in theological terms. But this may be merely its surface.

> We shall not cease from exploration
> And the end of all our exploring
> Will be to arrive where we started
> And know the place for the first time.

The language is imperative and oracular, but it gains its substance from its rhythmic control and its formal position within the whole sequence. Everything is mediated over its abstract surface, and its generality carries allusions to statements and beliefs rather than to objects and qualities. But to say that the poetry resides on this formal surface is to say that its power is derived from an ordered and rational aesthetic. The allusion of the quartets to music is very apt since, like music, the poetry offers the aesthetic gratification of form; it evokes and maintains a sensory appeal that makes persuasive or fluent the stated argument. It may seem paradoxical that Eliot creates a religious meaning out of the resources of an aesthetic formalism, but it is a necessary extension of Eliot's centrally humanist stance. For him, poetry offers the experience of certain meanings which will assure or elevate our sense of our selves. It was what has been recognised before in this analysis as Eliot's sense of the absorption of individual personality within a cultural 'tradition'. The idea of a Voice, rhetorical and impersonal, within the context of a formal aesthetic is one that can support that sense. The decision to dwell in form and not in language, in rhetoric and not in literature, is a decision for aesthetics. It is a decision that shapes Eliot's religious, as much as his social and political, thought. It is only necessary, at this point, to reaffirm the very different ability of Joyce to create a literature, thus moving outside the aesthetic realm of values. His work is 'formless' and 'meaningless' and this is precisely its strength. Perhaps where Eliot creates so strict an order of forms, the spaces that surround it become all the more tangible: spaces which are to be filled, not with the voices of men, but with the utterance of language.

This preoccupation with form, deriving as it does from a rationalist aesthetic, is of course one that runs deeply through the national culture. Auden, who refines and exploits a purely formal tradition, is the dominant presence and in certain writers who succeed him it simply becomes the easiest way to organise statements. It is not that there was a total weakening and restriction during this time: appearances are against such an easy formula. That access of self-consciousness in the birth of the "new" has in fact been noted already, and it is nowhere more evident than in the rise of the "new drama" of Osborne and Pinter, and in the rise of the "new novel" of writers like Braine and Sillitoe. There seemed to be a fresh current of force during the 'fifties which, by defining itself, overturned what was in contrast somehow the "old"; it is this force which should be brought to proper recognition, and the only way of doing this is to compare it with similar "new" movements in European culture.

Of course the argument must not be over-stated. The "new drama", as it was called, implies no revaluation of the consistency and theoretical intensity of, for example, the work of Mallarmé; it remained within those forms to which our culture had become accustomed, and within that human significance to which our culture has acceded. Zola had stated that "Au fond, le drame n'est donc qu'une étude de l'homme", which seems customary and trite enough until we recall Aristotle's very different description in the *Poetics*: "For tragedy is a representation, not of men, but of action and life, happiness and unhappiness." "Not of men . . .", it is this which strikes us as alien although the Aristotelian model has been the predominant one in western culture: a culture in which "men" only recently entered the dramatic world. But it is Zola's description which has become our own. That first 'revolutionary' play of the English stage, the one which initiated the "new drama", Osborne's *Look Back in Anger*, exists within its terms. And although English drama has developed beyond this point, it is instructive to see what seemed "new" in that recent period of our culture. It is a study of men, or rather of one man, Jimmy Porter. His dramatic locale is the familiar one, it is 'social reality': the curtain rises to disclose a "room", a space that imitates the real world. The fourth wall convention here is one that formulates the illusion of circumstantial reality; it is the one that locates at the same time as it confines the protagonists. The dramatic illusion of 'real life' is now so familiar that it hardly needs mentioning, but it is neither permanent nor universal; its force derives from a particular form of social consciousness and the work of Zola need only be recalled to recognise its implicit social determinism. The protagonists can only live in terms of their social and domestic interiors. In *Look Back In Anger*, Jimmy Porter learns through dramatic conflict that he cannot extricate himself from a confined and confining world: although it is actually Osborne's dramatic method that seals his fate.

This 'realism' has now become so much accepted that it has the status of myth. The limits of the "new" have already been fixed, and the drama of such "new" playwrights as Osborne and Pinter reaches back to the world of Bernard Shaw and beyond. The middle class world of Rattigan and Coward becomes, in the later "new" plays, a working class or 'bohemian' world but the formal, theatrical perspective of the 'fifties remains the same. Realism was taken for granted since it maintained the assumptions; in naturalistic theatre, the dramatic activity is focused upon certain human characters who take part in a certain action or story. This sounds like a parrot definition, and an unnecessary elucidation of what was everywhere apparent, but within the context of this analysis it becomes really quite eccentric and unusual. Who are these "characters" in Osborne? From his notes, certain fixed and determinate qualities are brought forward—Jimmy Porter, for example, is "a mixture of sincerity and cheerful malice"—but these qualities can only be mediated through an assured and rhetorical language. Osborne's characters exist solely in terms of their speech, and that speech possesses a rhetorical certainty and clarity which *is* their dramatic presence. At the centre of *Look Back In Anger* are the monologues of Jimmy Porter, which create themes of anger, nostalgia and isolation. "Jimmy" exists in terms of his passions:

> Hallelujah! I'm alive! I've an idea. Why don't we have a little game? Let's pretend that we're human beings, and that we're actually alive. Just for a while. What do you say? Let's pretend that we're human.

This is not a personal or individual voice; it is a self-evident and elaborate representation of private feeling, which claims authenticity in our response to its paradoxical fullness and certainty. The silences and broken sentences of Samuel Beckett's drama set in a new light the special formality of Osborne's early, "new" drama. He called his plays "lessons in feeling", and that is the central point. *Look Back in Anger* does not present argument or elicit judgement, it demands an emotional response. The audience is asked to participate in this 'real' action, and to identify itself with its rhetoric of feeling. In the words of one critic, Jimmy Porter "speaks as we would wish to" and Arnold Wesker once stated that "Art stirs the human spirit": what is shared here is the centrally humanist perspective of the 'fifties drama. It may take the form of a commitment to a certain kind of political action, and it may maintain the rationality and lucidity of action, but its origin does not lie there. It lies much further back, and the "new drama" stays a part of that revolutionary moment of the first modernism, when "human nature" first appeared under the guise of "experience" and "meaning".

But there is no real unity to the drama of the 'fifties. The plays of Harold Pinter, for example, are on the face of it less conventionally theatrical, and they are not conceived in such self-certainty. The characters of *The Caretaker*, to pick one of the more notorious examples, are dramatic precisely because they do not know themselves in the same way as a rhetorical construct like Jimmy Porter; and the circumstantial reality that Pinter creates is less substantial than Osborne's lucid world of feeling. Here, from *The Caretaker*, Aston asks Davies to take on the job as caretaker; it is their only moment of direct communication in the play:

> A. How do you feel about being one, then?
> D. Well I reckon. . . . Well I'd have to know, you know
> A. What sort of. . . .
> D. Yes what sort of . . . you know
> Pause
> A. Well, I mean. . . .
> D. I mean, I'd have to . . . I'd have to. . . .
> A. Well, I could tell you. . . .
> D. That's . . . that's it . . . you see . . . you get my meaning

This has none of the emotional range or lucidity of *Look Back in Anger*, it is not "as we would wish to speak". Pinter does not offer a rhetoric of feeling or the patterns of an idealised speech in order to encompass the world of the audience, but he makes his art out of hesitancies and trivial failures of personal speech. There is an impressionism, an elliptical quality that forms the play into a question, rather than a statement, of meaning. The audience does not participate in an action, it observes a state or mood. Although Pinter's plays, like those of Osborne, are conceived around the theme of personal isolation and sterility (this is a recurring theme at a time of declining subjectivity), he does not create a dramatic emotion out of conflict and change but a dramatic mood which exists outside the normal continuity and clarity of the drama. In his later plays, like *Landscape,* the 'reality' of circumstantial life disappears altogether and instead there are the passages of a wholly interior life:

> I would like to stand by the sea. It is there. . . .
> Pause
> I have. Many times. It's something I cared for. I've done it.
> Pause
> I'll stand on the beach. On the beach. Well . . . it was very fresh.

Here are the variations and inflections of the naked self. It is of course inevitable that Pinter should employ a fragmented lyricism to suggest private reveries, and at this late date it is naturally broken and incomplete. Drama is not literature, and its language cannot be expected to possess that self-sufficiency and autonomy which are to be discovered in the writings of Joyce. The language of drama is manipulated as an instrument of human meanings, and so it embodies all the ambiguities and failures of merely personal reference. In this sense, Pinter's dramas have always been quite orthodox, but it is an orthodoxy of some power when it can achieve that fullness which his best plays certainly have. There will, in fact, always be a creative and an effective orthodoxy and it will come to effect any eventual judgement which we will make about the progress of modernism.

How could modernism, which exists particularly within the written literature, be at all appropriate to drama? There is a reflection of it, at least, in the plays of Eugène Ionesco and the content of his plays certainly contradicts the humane and aesthetic significance which Osborne and Pinter share. Ionesco exploits the anti-naturalistic theatre of the Surrealists and the Theatre of Cruelty, but his anti-naturalism is very different from that of Pinter. In Pinter, the language—whether it is elliptical or simply lyrical—evokes private meanings and private responses; in Ionesco, the language forms itself into an opaque substance and dwells outside the characters who ostensibly mouth it. In *La Cantatrice*

Chauve, for example, the dialogue has nothing to do with any communicable meaning:

> She has regular features, but you can't call her beautiful. She's too tall and too well built. Her features are rather irregular, but everyone calls her beautiful. A trifle too short and too slight, perhaps.

In the absence of any dramatic and human meaning, the language itself becomes the subject of the plot in a grotesque parody of literature. We are again present in a universe of arbitrary speech:

> Said the barley to the cabbage, said the cabbage to the oats

appears within a dialogue, and 'communication' soon becomes nonsense:

> Krishnawallop, Krishnawallop, Krishnawallop.

Language comes to tyrannise over the protagonists. In another play, *La Leçon*, it is significant that the master is teaching the girl some form of comparative linguistics:

> Those who say, for example, in a Latin they take to be Spanish: "I've got pains in my chillblains" are as perfectly well understood by a Frenchman who doesn't know a word of Spanish.

And the master unleashes a torrent of nonsensical, or rather *autonomous* words that victimise the girl, until she is finally killed by the pronunciation of the word "knife". It is only a small twist to the theme of modernism that

> Arithmetic leads to Philology, and Philology leads to Crime.

This is a drama very different from the "new drama" which appeared at the same time in England. In Ionesco, that which is most real is not that which is most personal and most human: private identity is clouded by arbitrary language, and characters are identified only by external objects. His is not a drama of human truth or human passion (it would be impractical in an action in which characters change their names and their roles midway) and his plots do not claim that lucidity and continuity which we have come to expect of dramatic humanism. The plot may repeat itself or remain static, time sequences are deranged, and characters appear and disappear without recognisable motive. What is clearest and most substantial is simply the disembodied and opaque language of the play, which turns the project of an absolute literature into comedy.

The "new drama", in comparison, rests upon the national orthodoxy of 'reality' and 'meaning'. With its stage continuity and its human interaction, it presents an aesthetic illusion of life which is designed to be paradigmatic. That is what is meant by a public theatre. It moves through heightened emotional moments to elicit an emotional response from the audience, and the audience will confirm its own identity by sympathising with those characters who are peculiarly at the mercy of social circumstances. So England continues its long sleep in the first modernism.

At that same time as the "new drama" appeared, the "new novel" was announced and celebrated, and the work of Sillitoe, Storey and Braine was seen to be in the same community as that of Osborne and Pinter. It, too, transcribes a social world—and, more specifically, a class world; its style is the 'transparent' one which is designed to communicate a 'real' world of materials and objects. It is always the case with overtly naturalistic novels, of course, that fiction is rhetorically presented as fact: it deploys a range of external reference and a plain language so that it can create—just as it was created on the English stage—the aesthetic illusion of 'life' as it is commonly experienced. The style of *Saturday Night And Sunday Morning* or *Lucky Jim* is no different from that of the novels of Bennet or Galsworthy, and a new content is simply structured within an old form. The "new" novel was a novel of narrative and plot, character and motive, terms that keep their familiarity even at this late date. The great and recent success of detective novels is based upon an essential familiarity with these technical elements, since these particular texts display the formal mechanics of realistic fiction as their primary elements of meaning. They are the central texts of the twentieth-century social narrative.

John Braine's *Room At The Top*, although it has now been forgotten, was at the time praised as "new" and somehow representative, and twenty years on it may serve some purpose to see which face our culture regarded as its own. The novel begins with a first person narrative: "I came to Warley on a wet September morning," and that "I", Joe Lampton, dominates the whole novel. He is a "working class" man arriving in a middle class environment: "I was certain I was in the presence of a thousand a year," and his character comes to be representative, or at least recognisable, only in the terms of his social milieu. Braine constructs a fiction of the way 'things are', and his apparent verisimilitude is conveyed by the detailed description of towns, streets, conversations—all, of course, features of a social reality and all of them mediated through the authorial "I" of the narrative. It is an "I" sustained by an ordered plot which has a beginning, a middle and an end; the narrative establishes an aesthetic law which, in turn, sustains the characters who mouth recognisable passions within an ordered speech:

> She started to cry again. "Oh God, you're so normal, I do love you for that. I do love you. I do love you. . . ." She spoke the next words in a whisper, "I'm so happy with you that I wish I could die now."

Here is the last claim of aesthetic prose, in which a 'realistic' narrative generates lucid passions and typical responses as though they are to be conceived factually. The readers are sustained by a clear and comforting sense of themselves.

But this is merely the narrative surface of the novel, and the interior life of *Room At The Top* is more irresolute and troubling: for reasons that have to do with the authorial "I" which orders the narrative in terms of its own significance. The "I" sees the action in retrospect and from a position of superiority. It is an "I" that determines and objectifies itself within the narrative; there is, in fact, a continual, studied impersonality which places the "I" apart from itself: "I didn't like Joe Lampton" and, again of himself, "He was of a higher quality then, he could feel more, he could take more strain."

This has very little to do with the apparent plot of Joe Lampton's rise into an inauthentic self. It is a question of the false subjectivity which Braine must impose upon his narrative in order to manage its content. The authorial "I" denies itself by turning itself into an object of the action which it describes. It dehumanises itself, and thus places the status of the whole narrative in doubt. A false subjectivity radiates into the objects which it sets off against

itself: the other characters in the novel are either treated as stereo-
types (the business men, the 'theatrical' people) or are conceived
sentimentally (as Susan is within the narrative). The people become
things to be displayed around the subject—Lampton always talks
of the business men, for example, as "zombies"—and so depict
the implicit structure of the novel. The death of Joe's lover, Alice,
"a lump of raw meat with the bones sticking through" imitates
at a thematic level the central dispensation of the writing. Everything is mediated through a false "I", and the writing is turned
into a clumsy instrument for its expression. It is self-conscious:
"Perhaps that sounds portentous, but let it stand" and melo-
dramatic: "In a queer but pleasurable way it actually hurt me to
look at her. I fell in love with her at first sight." The writing
depicts the inauthenticity and impersonality of its "I" by attempt-
ing to objectify itself: ". . . my intentions toward Susan were those
which are described an honourable," in the manner in which
everything is hardened into types and roles. The aesthetic confusion of fiction and fact is here illustrated in its purest form.

The prose novel has characteristically been the medium for
communicating the language of social and human relations (it is
not an accidental critical cliché that the age of the first modernism
is known as the "Age of Prose"), but it is a form which has slack-
ened in our own time. The social novel had already narrowed
down, in writers like Braine, to the sphere of the problematic "I"
and its techniques, and it has now become a form that lies dorm-
ant within its own historicity. It could not be in greater contrast
to the French "nouveau roman", which emerged at the same time
as the "new novel" in England. The French writers had a typically
analytical and theoretical bent which, although it may seem mis-
placed in terms of creative writing, is one that propelled the novel
out of its literary past and into a new awareness of what it is to
express the "social" and the "human".

Alain Robbe-Grillet's *Les Gommes* was published in 1953, and
it marked the beginning of a new writing, and its particular originality has in part already been analysed in a theoretical study which
Robbe-Grillet has written, entitled *Pour Un Nouveau Roman*. There
is a central emphasis in this essay on the disappearance of the
novel as a realistic fiction, as an aesthetic mediator between man

and the world; the novel is to excise its humanist strategies, since Robbe-Grillet no longer sees the form as a vehicle for the imposition of a subjective or human significance upon the world. Since it no longer offers a malleable world, the authorial "I" or "he" must disappear, together with those *topoi* of "character" and "plot" which suggest an unreal continuity and omniscience.

Robbe-Grillet's *La Jalousie*, for example, is a narrative of suspected adultery and submerged passion. But this passage from it evokes the contours of the narrative on very different principles from those which its apparent themes might suggest. It is the description of a song:

> If the themes sometimes blur, they only recur somewhat later, all the more clearly, virtually identical. Yet these repetitions, these tiny variations, halts, regressions, can give rise to modifications—though barely perceptible—eventually moving quite far from the point of departure.
>
> To hear better, A . . . has turned her head towards the open window next to her.

The even and syntactically subtle descriptive manner here evokes the whole tenor of Robbe-Grillet's narrative, just as the ostensible content makes an elliptical reference to its concealed and gradual movement. The central theme of *La Jalousie* is the process of invention itself, radiating in this passage from an observer who can only be assumed, and all of Robbe-Grillet's writing dramatises the obsessive and mechanical dimensions of the creative process. Time, as in the song, does not move lineally but exists only within the duration of the composition, as a recurring pattern or as an infinitely plastic medium. There is no plot that proceeds from beginning to end, thus imitating natural growth and decay, but a pattern of movement in which, like the song, "everything might stop without warning".

The aesthetic of *Room At The Top* was one in which fictional variables emerge within certain factual constants, thus allowing the reader to become implicated in the fiction and reassuring him that his life is not devoid of meaning or rational continuity. For Robbe-Grillet, fiction is simply fiction, and it reaches its highest

THE USES OF HUMANISM

point in a steadfast denial of the 'real' world, which can only be described as that which impinges when one has stopped reading. His is a literature and not a rhetoric. So how can his fiction redeem the social world? By refusing to possess or to control it. And how can his fiction redeem subjectivity? By refusing to make it a type, or a character within the lucid terms of naturalism. Although Robbe-Grillet's novels dramatise a subject's creation of meaning, no "I" ever appears and what is given instead is a neutral, descriptive style. It dwells on the surface of planes and solids, of events and of people:

> The sentences followed one another, each in its place, connecting locally. The measured, uniform tone was like that of a witness offering testimony or a recitation.

> "Even so," A . . . says, "you thought you could fix it yourself at first. At least you tried."

> She smiles as she says these last words. They look at each other. He smiles too.

Here is a scene described by an unheard and unseen observer, in which adultery and passion are the ostensible references. But there is no interior analysis, only the resonant movement of the surface of things, in their displacement and their habitual presence. There is no fixed meaning or plot to be deciphered, but there is rather a sense of expectation and unfamiliarity since meaning is being continually created. It takes a complete reading of the text to uncover this continual accumulation and shifting of meaning, and it eventually creates a sense of a world which stands apart from our own efforts to impart significance to it. What is being offered is the bland and precise aspect of things. Even though the novel is conceived in terms of a passionate consciousness that sees and describes, it is not one that can structure the world in order to project its own meaning upon it.

What, in fact, is this consciousness which is not even an "I" but which mediates the narrative: Robbe-Grillet has talked of his novel as being "subjective", but who is the subject? Who is it that is talking? It may be 'the husband' in *La Jalousie*, and Mathias the sexual psychotic in *Le Voyeur*. But these are not types who are being used to characterise a passion, or who are full of passions, since it is only by means of their continual scrutiny of the world that their meaning is delivered to us. Where John Braine has to define and describe feeling through metaphor and authorial statement, the subjectivity which Robbe-Grillet creates is one that is delivered through the direct transcription of what is placed before it. There is no plot to act as an accomplice to the characters' expression of "love", "anger" and the other names; there is only the sense of the world as being both itself and, within the fiction, of a material density which relates to consciousness only in the act of being seen.

Obsessions are located in repeated patterns that emerge, in the need to measure and to precisely locate. It comes close to that earlier and more philosophical description of intentional consciousness, in which objects appear only in relation to a living consciousness just as consciousness itself only exists in the context of that object which it perceives. The central activity of Robbe-Grillet's writing has its place here. For obsessions feed upon the attempt to impose an inner order and meaning upon the world, although it is within the very curve of this obsession that the objects of the world emerge and stay apart from ourselves and our needs. Appearances are unassailable and ambiguous, and they are not to be tied down. It is when this is recognised, when they are not warped to encircle the 'hero' and to echo his cries, that their particular life emerges. Again, the subjective consciousness only fulfils its potential when it is seen to exist in the act of meaning itself, and not as a medium for certain conventional truths and inherited utterances. Only when the aesthetic of humanism has been excised can both the social and the personal worlds emerge into their own being. The "nouveau roman" is one that creates literature, because it sees fiction as fiction and not as truth.

(2) Aesthetic Humanism

There is at least one European movement that has affected English criticism, and it has been that of 'structuralism'. For some it is simply a fashionable discipline to be studied at university, and

106

for others it has developed into a critical positivism through which all texts can be scrutinised and placed. But its alignments are neither as vague nor as grandiose as they have appeared; structuralism did not spring, fully armed, upon literary academics and its role has been an essential but minor one in the movement which has gone from the texts of Nietzsche to those of the phenomenologists. The most notable exponent of structuralism has been Claude Levi-Strauss, and his work will reveal most of its particular strategies. What is, for example, the context of structuralism? In *Tristes Topiques*, an autobiographical study, Levi-Strauss states that "its mission is to understand Being in relation to itself, not in relation to oneself" since it is a discipline fundamentally extrinsic to the claims of subjectivity. Subjective experience had already been redefined in the investigations of phenomenology, but Levi-Strauss takes an absolute stand outside the context of experience. In *Tristes Topiques*, he makes this clear: "Phenomenology I found unacceptable because it postulated a continuity between experience and reality;" again, he repeats the objection that has already been raised against existentialism: ". . . it is the exact opposite of true thought by reason of its indulgent attitude toward the illusions of subjectivity."

What, then, are the resources of a methodology which excises subjectivity, and which can claim a truth as permanent as that of Levi-Strauss's "three mistresses", Marxism, geology and psychoanalysis? There may be some guidance to be found in the writings of Durkheim, who to a certain extent anticipates Levi-Strauss. Durkheim's concept of "collective representation", the permanent ground of his sociology, is of one that "exists outside the individual consciousness" and operates upon it "coercively". But Durkheim's is an anthropology since it exists within the space of man and his actions: and it is this space which Levi-Strauss abandons. So what is the context of his own enquiry, an enquiry which is to both absolute and alien to man? It can only be that one which literature first discloses, and against which all sociology and phenomenology are formulated: the truth which Levi-Strauss affirms beyond subjectivity, and the model to which he admits his first inspiration, is that of an absolute language. His ideological debt to De Saussure, the founder of modern linguistics, is the profound one and the continuing metaphor in Levi-Strauss's work is that of the absolute and arbitrary structures of language to which man clings. In his 'Ouverture' to *Raw And Cooked*, Levi-Strauss puts it thus: "I have tried to give an outline of the syntax of South American mythology." What structuralism claims as its context is this "syntax", this form of knowledge which displaces humanism and has already been described in this analysis as the emergence of language.

Levi-Strauss's constant effort is to disclose a "truth" outside the immediate and unmediated facts of experience. He states in *Raw And Cooked* that "I have always aimed at drawing up an inventory of mental patterns, to reduce apparently arbitrary data to some kind of order, and to attain a level at which a kind of necessity becomes apparent." By rendering apparent and observable what was once unconscious or undisclosed within experience, Levi-Strauss claims for his enquiry a permanence and a universality. But it is not a 'content' that he discloses, in a new truth or exegesis, but a methodology. He locates those formal properties which structure any content whatsoever: "Structure has no distinct content: it is the content itself, apprehended as a logical organisation which is conceived as a property of the real." But what are these formal properties which do not stand apart from matter, but which permeate it as its necessary properties? In his essay, *Structural Linguistics*, Levi-Strauss postulates them as those which he had found already in use in structural linguistics: ". . . not conscious phenomena, but unconscious superstructure, not terms but the relation between terms, the concept of system and the discovery of general laws." It is necessary to recognise in this context how heavily Levi-Strauss depends upon the techniques of the linguist, Roman Jakobson. His account of kinship systems, for example, is based upon Jakobson's binary linguistic model, which constructs a system of oppositions into which any code can be deconstructed. The dubiety of Jakobson's model is not in question here, but what is important is that pressure towards absolute description which determines the force and the scope of Levi-Strauss's writings. His concern, in a text like *The Savage Mind*, is to discover the formal conditions "necessary for any significant message to be conveyed . . . and to guarantee the convertibility of ideas between different levels of social reality".

"Content" is evoked here only to appear as the particular "message" or social code, and it has lost that anthropocentric status as the realm in which man discovers and comforts himself. In fact, structuralism, in its disavowal of content, resides in that space which Mallarmé and Nietzsche first open and it is, in part, a technical development out of literature. It is, of course, a method that is designed to cover all social phenomena and all forms of symbolic exchange, but the written language is the most arbitrary and the most permanent of all types of that exchange. It is not an historical accident that structuralism should first come to light as semiology, or the science of signs, and that it should be anticipated by Ferdinand De Saussure, who formalises and describes the emergence of language.

De Saussure's *The Uses of Language* is a primary source of structural method. His posthumous notes, published as *Cours du Linguistique Générale*, develop and extend into a technical form that first access of modernism in the work of Mallarmé and Nietzsche. The last sentence of the *Cours* is "The true and unique object of linguistics is language studied in and for itself;" language is a self-contained whole to be studied by an autonomous science. It is "collective . . . it is essential . . . it is homogeneous . . . it is not a function of the speaker, it is a product that is passively assimilated by the speaker" and this is the first technical formulation of the absolute entity which displaces the claims of humanism and which structuralism later claims as the model of its enquiry. It is in this context, also, that De Saussure makes the central distinction between the permanent form of language, "langue", and "langage", the individual speech which it generates and also maintains. It is this distinction which is crucial to Levi-Strauss's attempt to transcend immediate experience by discovering the formal properties which constitute it. De Saussure goes on to state that language "is a form and not a substance"; it has no content but content can only emerge through it. It is with this absoluteness that the self-referentiality of language is again described: "the linguistic sign is arbitrary" since there is no necessary relation between the signifier (the sign or acoustic image) and the signified

109

(the concept or sense content which it points toward). Although it was originally part of a contractual arrangement, "the distinguishing characteristic of the sign is that it in some way always eludes the individual or social will". Language exists as a system of oppositions and relations prior to subjectivity and to experience, and as an entity that has no content. All of these themes come to be used in structuralist thought.

But I want to return briefly to a different matter. The absence or denial of "content" in language is one that was described in the first chapter of this analysis as fostering the birth of what was, literally, "nothing"—in orthodox rationalist terms. Literature, like De Saussure's "langue", has no content. It is established, as we have discovered, upon its absence; and it is this absence which De Saussure formulates as the concept of "difference". Like Nietzsche, he asserts that language has no content but contains only differences. Language, that is, is maintained by the differential relations between signs (they can only be recognised in terms of their difference between one another), and it consists of a network of extrinsic relations: ". . . in language there are only differences without positive terms." In the Port-Royal *Logique* the emphasis had rested solely upon what is positive and perfectly evident, but now in De Saussure there is a no less technical formulation of the reverse significance. It is the significance of a form, a series of relations, that is immanent but undisclosed. I was going to say, that is "unconscious", but this will require further analysis: the "unconscious" appears as an entity soon after the emergence of language, and they have a close relation.

So it is the central distinction of form and experience that Levi-Strauss transposes from linguistic method, and it is a distinction that he develops in his sense of structuralist method as uncovering the laws of opposition and relation which underlie all the codes of conscious life. His sense of form is one, in fact, that belongs —crucially—to the domain of the unconscious as it was first described by Sigmund Freud. The unconscious, for Levi-Strauss, is the permanent ground for the structural relations which he will disclose and it can also claim exactly that permanence and necessity which he was seeking in his construction of a method. The French psychologist, Jaques Lacan, confirms the role of the unconscious in structuralist theory in *The Repetition Of The Letter*: ". . . the psychoanalytic experience discovers in the unconscious the whole structure of language." And, in the Freudian interpretation of dreams, "it is only the signifier that is important, not the signified". The domain of language is slowly being extended.

The connection of language and the unconscious, on whatever terms we describe it, is central to structuralist method. The unconscious is, for Levi-Strauss, the universal form which gives signification to content although it is itself content-less. Like language as De Saussure understood it, it is not substance but form. Like language, too, it contains no "meanings" but is simply that system of relations which is projected into conscious life and speech. These ideas are very far removed from the radiant rationalism of the humanists, within the lucidity of which Man can preserve himself. Language and the unconscious become the necessary condition for the relations between self and the world, although they themselves exist beyond the area of immediate experience; they constitute what is intelligible within "content" although they both continually escape the scrutiny of consciousness and can be located only as the principle of difference, as being other than what we perceive. Nietzsche's hypothesis of the "text" which has forever been lost, but which is always the ground of interpretation, is compatible here. This is the dominant image of modernism, and it is the one which irradiates structuralist thought.

The unconscious gives meaning, but is itself meaningless, just as language is without content but projects the laws of content. Their relation has been recognised before, but always on misleading terms; the Surrealists, for example, construct a "language of the unconscious" or a "stream of consciousness", when these concepts actually vitiate the nature of both language and the unconscious by describing them in terms of a "content" and in terms of individual creativity. It is only within structuralist method that their actual primacy and the actual terms of their inter-relation can come into play, since they act as the principles through which social and private experience can be deconstructed.

It is at this point that the work of Roland Barthes comes into its own, since he is not the first but the most substantial of the structuralist literary critics. The critical emphasis of his writing is clear, since it is that which was popularised in the writings of Levi-Strauss; Barthes proposes a general formula in *Essais Critiques*: "Le but de tout activité structuraliste est de reconstituer un 'objet' de facon à manifester dans cette reconstitution les règles de fonctionnement de cet objet." The borrowing from the modernist tradition is much in evidence here, and Barthes' interest in the "objet" is reminiscent of Jakobson's formula that the poem has structural levels which relate "to give the poem the nature of an absolute object". And there is a strengthening of this relation between linguistics and structuralist criticism in Barthes' essay, *Eléments de Sémiologie*, which takes the work of De Saussure as its inspirational centre. This emphasis is continued in Barthes' account of criticism as "the meta-language of literature", and of literature itself as "the science of language". He confirms the study of literature as an autonomous entity, a concept which has been growing in strength and reference throughout this analysis.

Barthes sees his role as critic as that of deconstructing a system of signs "which takes as its object not its content but its own form". This disavowal of content has now become a familiar one, but its absence is constituted within these "signs". For Barthes, writing is the primary manifestation of language; he is clearer about this than Levi-Strauss. For although Levi-Strauss could only derive his notion of autonomous and arbitrary structure from the written form of language, he continually suggests that he is working from a structure of spoken or phonetic oppositions. This confusion between the spoken and written variants of language creates great ambiguity in the study of linguistics itself; in the work of Levi-Strauss, for example, it causes some confusion between arbitrary social models and the immediacy of individual life. But for Barthes, the form of literature is contained within the act of writing, and no longer in those "of 'thinking', 'portraying', 'telling' or 'feeling'." This is not an emphasis which comes easily to us, but it may seem less eccentric when placed beside a similar statement in the notebooks of Wittgenstein. Together, they suggest that community of response which the birth of language has evoked: "There is a kind of general disease of thinking which always looks for and finds what could be called a mental state, from which all our acts spring as from a reservoir." And again: "Understanding a sentence means getting hold of its content; and the content of the sentence is *in* the sentence." This deconstruction of any inner/outer dichotomy—language is no longer to be taken as 'expressive'—is not one entirely foreign to structuralist method. When Carnap explains that "philosophy is the syntax of the language of science" we may be in a different area from that of Levi-Strauss's disclosure of "the syntax of South American mythology", but the common allusion locates the essential common ground of their enquiries.

This community of interest does not mean, of course, that Barthes' writing lies within a static or simplistic system; structuralism is an activity and not a metaphysic, and there are changes of emphasis as well as a general development. In the criticism of Barthes, for example, the "objectness" of the poem is not as certain as it appears to be in Jakobson's analysis, nor does it have quite the painstaking lucidity of Levi-Strauss's mythic structures: Barthes' description of literary structures has that same ambiguity and indefiniteness which accrues to the still unfamiliar idea of autonomous literature. The poem, or rather the "text", is not self-contained or "sui-referential" in an orthodox sense. In Barthes' essay, *S/Z*, an account of Balzac, there is a description which is important in this context: ". . . ce texte est un galaxie de signifiants, non une structure de signifiés . . . il est renversible . . . les codes qu'il mobilise so profile à perte de vue, ils sont indécidables."

According to Barthes, there is in any work a continually shifting and unstable aggregation of social codes and individual messages, which exist at different levels within the texts which contain them. This does not in the least resemble Jakobson's description of discrete levels of "phonetic" and "semantic" meaning, and has rather more to do with what Barthes calls "l'être de la pluralité" and "textes multivalents". Once again the spirit of Nietzsche's enquiry into multiplicity and difference is in evidence—and could it be that structuralist method embodies Nietzsche's dream, the exegesis of exegesis itself?

What, then, is the function of structuralist analysis when faced with the irretrievable multiplicity of the text? According to Barthes, its aim is to deconstruct the act of reading itself: "le décomposition du travail de lecture . . . le commentateur trace le long du texte des zones de lecteur afin d'y observer la migration du sense, l'affleurement des codes, le passage des citations." The analysis of the experience of reading discloses a plurality of codes, and of voices that function by contrast and opposition. But the act of reading cannot be seen as qualitatively different from the internal relations of the text itself, since it does not presume a phenomenological description established upon a pure act of consciousness. The text exists in relation only to "itself" and not to "me": ". . . les sens que je trouve sont avérés, non par 'moi' ou d'autres mais par leur marque systematique." The act of reading does not consist of the subjective experience of an object— which is the fundamental principle of aesthetics—but rather of the relation between one text and another: ". . . la subjectivité n'est que le sillage de tous les codes qui me font," so that the perspective of written language has completely usurped the claims of the selfhood. Barthes' structuralism transcends the dichotomy of subject and object on much the same terms as Nietzsche's analysis; there is no permanent or standard value, there is only an attempt "d'affirmer l'être de la pluralité, qui n'est pas celui du vrai." In this sense, Barthes can overturn the conventional categories of 'poem' and 'novel', together with that no less conventional category of 'I', and can allow the 'text' to emerge as the object of knowledge. If we had read Barthes in a partial perspective, his account of criticism as the act of reading would have seemed suspiciously like a simplistic version of phenomenology, but Barthes sees that 'we' are, in our reading, accomplices in the autonomy of language. We, too, are texts to be deconstructed and Barthes anticipates, more clearly than the writers who have preceded him, the fall of the idea of "Man".

This denial of human "nature" is, of course, subversive within the Anglo-Saxon tradition, where the self-evident truths of humanism have appeared under the guises of naturalism and formalism. But this cannot be a simple or categorical matter. There is in the critical work of F. R. Leavis, for example, a complex discovery of the English 'tradition'. His general humanism has already been defined: it is his sense of human experience and of moral competence imparting significance and subtlety to the language. And it is this sense which Leavis develops in his later writings, from *The Common Pursuit*, published in 1952, to *Pluralism, Compassion And Social Hope*. This last title suggests the extension of Leavis's public interests, but his understanding of the literature is the crucial matter to be raised. Leavis imparts a particular emphasis which we have now seen to be customary within our national culture: "To have a living literature is to have an informing spirit in civilisation, an informed, charged and authoritative awareness of inner human nature and human need." There are to be these permanent meanings which reside outside language, but which language is to embody and to continue; "human nature" is the ambiguous figure behind all the enquiry, and it remains the touchstone of relevance.

Leavis's position is much more subtle and elusive than this précis, but the main lines of his argument are here. He is not concerned with Quiller-Couch's sense of literature as a "storehouse of values", but with the "collaborative interplay" within the language in response to a literature which "creates the essential values and significances of the human world". It is paradoxical that literature should be seen to "create" human values, and I want to return later to this apparent reversal of terms. Leavis understands literature as a dialectic between "abstract" thought and "concrete" experience, and he responds in part to the reformed status of language by describing it as "the essential life of a culture . . . for community and change", in its role of being one and many, both self and others. This is close to the phenomenological description of speech, and it represents a notable development from Leavis's earlier sense of language as embodying "feelings and emotions". But the context is still one of external and utilitarian value; literature is to denote the human world and its values which, although they can only be brought to proper life and relevance through expression, are not necessarily integral to it.

These values are extrinsic. Leavis's version of social history continually assumes their presence, since they are what is being threatened and destroyed by "technologico-Benthamite" civilisation since "it is a matter of innermost human nature being thwarted and starved." Here he has been anticipated by Matthew Arnold, who states the central, humanist position: "man is not

115

to be civilised or humanised by thwarting his vital instincts;" part of Arnold's response to a dehumanised society is "in substituting poetry for religion" (*On Translating Homer*) which suggests an even more strongly utilitarian stance than that of Leavis himself. In Leavis's own writings, his sense of "the traditional culture" is lent a descriptive force and a context of organic metaphor which stress its consonance with "innermost human nature". But this culture has been lost, in Leavis's analysis, at the time of a split between an "educated" and "popular" public, and was finally disoriented by the 'industrial revolution'. When he talks of a "breach of continuity", he is actually describing a central displacement of human nature. If we are to question this position, we need not concern ourselves with Leavis's historical analysis, or with his unexplored analogy between "human nature" and "traditional culture". The significant point is that these values are actually to be derived from a reading of literature, and that they are thus fundamentally aesthetic values.

For Leavis, it is only within literary texts that certain necessary qualities can be recognised and recovered: "English literature gives us a continuity that is not yet dead . . . there is no other access to anything approaching a full continuity of mind, spirit and sensibility—which is what we desperately need." It is with this sense of literature as imparting a continuity to human values that Leavis can treat it as a diagnostic and didactic force: it can "do something important towards remedying those disorders of civilised life which frighten us". As in Arnold, the humanist conception of literature is one that finally claims a *use* for it within the social world.

This is the general thematic surface of Leavis's work, this humanism which asserts an equivalence of "literature" and "life" (with much the same prescriptive force as the 'realism' of a writer like John Braine), but it is in the actual texture of Leavis's writing that his prevailing aestheticism comes into play. It is not simply that his description of literature is one that takes as its centre a human content, but that the values he ascribes to literature— "complexity" and "organic inter-relatedness", for example—are exactly those qualities which Leavis demands from a culture and a human society. When Leavis talks of literature as "a cultural

116

community or consciousness", he is not being metaphoric: he is affirming an identity of literary and social values. "What matters for each age is coherence," and it was exactly that need for coherence which he had first affirmed in his analysis of the English novel. Again, "there can be no national greatness when there is no strong spiritual continuity", although continuity itself had first been assumed as the criterion of a rationalist aesthetic. This is the strange alchemy of humanism, in which aesthetic standards can be transformed into spiritual and social needs. When Leavis makes a moral evaluation of the quality of individual life which is being starved by industrialisation, it has great force: ". . . the livingness of the deepest vital intelligence, a power—rooted, strong in experience and supremely human", but he is repeating in a generalised, ethical context what was once the particular analysis of good poetry: ". . . subtlety, flexibility and complexity." The identity of concerns is quite evident. When Leavis asserts the need for recapturing "end" and "significance", he is not simply asking that literary judgements be judgements also about life, he is operating in an aesthetic context which reifies these judgements until they become the sole criteria for what is and what is not valuable.

In this sense, Leavis's description of the collapse of "traditional culture" becomes, at its most important level, a lamentation for the collapse of a humane aesthetic, since it represents the disintegration of that fullness of sensory gratification which is the ground for an idealised "organic community". Leavis's sense of "unity", "continuity" and "significance" are not the necessary conditions for optimum life on earth, they are rather the generalisations of an old aesthetic. His morality of aesthetic imposes a false significance upon "life", and so life readily evades his grasp. Leavis had the courage and perspicacity to locate a giant transition, but it was not within the nature of his humanism to recognise it as anything other than a loss.

It is in this light that the English literary criticism of the 'fifties can best be read. It became known as a kind of "sociological" criticism, and its most notable exponent is Raymond Williams. The adjective is vague; if it is traced back to its origin in the writings of Durkheim, it reaffirms the truth of *homo humanus*, object of its study, which exists outside language. And it is in fact within this generalised anthropology that the writings of Williams find their place, and also where their affinity with the writings of Leavis can be best recognised. Williams's description of art in *The Long Revolution* is indicative: ". . . communication is the crux of art . . . it is the organisation of experience." Again, "to succeed in art is to convey an experience to others in such a way that the experience is actively recreated". And, in another context, a novel is described as "the dramatisation of values".

This very clumsy location of "experience" and "values" within literature is a familiar one, whose sources no longer need to be elucidated. It is part of that humanism, which Leavis shares, which postulates the truth-giving and didactic powers of literature. In Williams's description, novels "offer us a truth about ourselves" and they are "for defining human society rather than merely reflecting it". The written language embodies certain values which are extrinsic to it, and which refer to our "common life". Thus, Williams's methodology in *Culture And Society* is to deconstruct certain texts in terms of "culture", "art" and "society" and so to reaffirm the status of these texts within the human and socialised world. Their common origin is a "thinking about community" and in *The Novel from Dickens to Lawrence* it is this sense of community which is seen as the touchstone for response and judgement. But what is the "community"? Williams has many analogies for it: ". . . we need a common culture . . . a genuine common experience . . . an equality of being." And where else can we recover these necessary values but in the experience of literature: ". . . most novels are in a sense knowable communities." This is the central definition and we can chart, as we did in Leavis, Williams's critical response to language being gradually transformed into the context for moral and social judgements. Just as a rational aesthetic allows man to know himself within an area of "significance" and "continuity", so Williams's "knowable community" is a way of creating an antithesis to individualism while at the same time retaining the status of individual creation. This strategy comes into effect, too, in Williams's discovery of a "structure of feeling" within the novel; it is apparently a formalism which is designed to sustain a subjective content, but this "structure of feeling" soon becomes extended: "This structure of feeling is the culture of the period . . . the new generation will have its own structure of feeling." The idea of community has now become a literary and aesthetic one.

The social emphasis of Williams's aesthetic comes into full play in *Modern Tragedy*. It is here that he puts my central argument for me: "If we find a particular idea of tragedy in our time, we find also a way of interpreting a very wide area of experience." A reading of literature provides a way of describing and defining "experience"; this is the domain of literary humanism. When Williams talks of certain "permanent and universal meanings in our experience", it is important to be sceptical of a "meaning" that has so bookish an origin. Just as with "community", Williams creates "meaning" from a confusion between aesthetic qualities and the nature of life-experience. It had been exactly that confusion which Husserl had cleared some fifty years earlier, in his redefinition of experience. The permanent theme of this analysis has been the disappearance of humanism and of aesthetics, as the distinction between language and experience became clearer and clearer. To see "revolution in a tragic perspective", as Williams does, is to reverse this development and to raise aesthetics into a morality.

Leavis and Williams are formative influences within the academic study of literature; and faced with the paucity and decline within the English departments of the universities, we must look to the common assumptions of these two critics. In their essential form, they are the strategies of a late version of orthodox humanism: it seeks for values through which it can affirm itself in certain literary texts, although it ignores the problematic idea of literature and does not recognise the ascendant status of language within it. It tries to take from literature what literature cannot provide—the ability to constitute an ideology of action. From a false notion of literature is generated a false notion of 'life' and 'community', and our culture suffers. There has still been no significant change.

119

6

The Pursuit of Modernism

ὡς γὰρ ἐπεκλώσαντο θεοὶ δειλοῖσι βροτοῖσιν
ζώειν ἀχνύμενους αὐτὸι δέ τ' ακηδέες εἰσίν
Homer: *The Iliad*

The situation of criticism, as it has been outlined here, does not of course have any direct reference to the creative writing of our time; there exists only a common concern, and a common capacity for certain kinds of discourse. The related values of humanism and subjectivity have been seen to be the ground of Anglo-Saxon criticism, since these are the values which represent that knowledge which lies to the far side of language and the general movement of modernism. And it is in this spirit that the confusions and weakness of our recent creative achievement become comprehensible: I want to turn to some examples of recent poetry, and particularly to the "new poetry" of the last decade, which now constitutes an 'establishment' writing and which has become most popular in the work of Sylvia Plath and Ted Hughes. If there is to be one immediate function of this analysis, it is to rid these poets of a false terminology of the "new".

The poetry of Plath is a poetry of theme, and of mood. It has a content which structures it, and gives it force: it has been described as the poetry of 'breakdown' and this does evoke the pervasive, personal direction of the poetry. The content is engineered by a single voice, which becomes most immediate in certain varities of description:

> And I saw white maggots coil
> Thin as pins in the dark bruise,
> Where his innards bulged

120

It is the characteristic quality of this poetry that the description claims no false 'symbolic' or 'imagistic' potential; it tends towards the visual, or toward the plain statement of effect. Metaphor and analogy exist on the unmediated surface of the language without claiming any structural or thematic coherence: you might say that they are merely applied within the assertive movement of the line, and it is in this bland application that the 'voice' of the poem can be found.

The tone of Sylvia Plath within her poetry is a dominant, personal one; it is the self at its most transparent, without the resources of irony or inherited discourse. It is described as the poetry of "breakdown", but this is the necessary delimitation—at this late date—of the subjective voice. The tradition of the personal is at its weakest and most vulnerable point:

> How they grip us through thin and thick
> The barnacle dead

> They are always with us, the thin people
> Meagre of dimension as the grey people

The slightness of the forms here, and the simple assertiveness of their statements, suggest that narrowness of voice offering a singleness of content. The potential effectiveness of the theme is submerged and flattened by the paucity of the movement of the line. But it is not in the least strange that the language of "extremity" should also be the language of cliché, since they are both rooted in the weak and declining principle of moral "experience".

The language of these poems is entirely referential. It is responsive to "feeling" and to thematic experience rather than to itself, and so it remains a weak, mimetic force. There is an attempt within Sylvia Plath's poetry to describe and to recreate 'meaning' and certain emotional 'truths', but this is at the cost of turning language into a mere instrument. It is narrowed down into a blunt force:

> Nigger-eye
> Berries cast dark
> Hooks

121

where the quality of the poetry resides in its denotative potential, each word being pressed to secrete a force and a weight. But there can be no 'experience' behind this denotative language; the heavy differentiation of each syllable and phrase breaks the language apart, and reduces it to a set of counters and ciphers of meaning; thematic continuity can then only be arranged by the conventional devices of alliteration and onomatopeia:

> I am ill
> I have taken a pill to kill

since these devices operate on the rhetorical surface of language, in a writing in which every aspect has been reduced to a tool of private meaning.

The central weakness of such private meaning is one that comes forward on a thematic level, since the experience of the self is, for Plath, one of disintegration. Thumb, throat, bone and other parts of the body seem to float free and exist within their own space. They become the objective elements of a false subjectivity:

> Scorched to the root,
> My red filaments burn and stand, a hand of wires

Everything is hard and lifeless within this fixed language, because the experience of a false subjectivity generates a false world of objects. But the subjective world is one, too, that resides in certain values: in a sense of human truth and content. What the poetry of Plath offers, in particular, is an aesthetic of despair. This is the 'meaning' which her writing denotes, and what is more enjoyable than despair? The sense of breakdown and horror which the "new poetry" generated is a simple inversion of orthodox humanist values, and it is no less close to them. We are asked to participate in the progress of the poem, with its extrinsic reference and assertive movement, and to find ourselves within its content; it is diagnostic, at the limits of the personal. But this most 'private' of poets is at the same time one of the most accessible.

There is an analogy with the verse of Ted Hughes, who enjoys a similar popularity despite his withdrawal into private meanings. His writing is one that has inherited larger resources than that of Plath; it is not that it questions itself, or raises the language into

the subject of the poem, but rather that it has acquired a number
of rhetorical and technical devices which segregate it from other
forms of language:

> His wings hold all creation in a weightless space,
> Steady as a hallucination in the streaming air.

It is a more controlled and a more substantial language than that
of Plath, because it does not rest so completely upon a private
voice. Its movement is larger, and there is a continuity and a harmony which derive from a formal ability to control the statements.
But it is also an assertive poetry which organises itself around a
human content, and around certain obvious themes; we must
assume the status of the poem and its single 'voice' in order to
focus upon the moral experience that is being recreated for us.
The dwelling upon what is extrinsic makes for a rhetoric of feeling:

> His palace is of skulls

> His crown is the last splinters
> Of the vessel of life

and the resources of metaphor and analogy have a purely technical
role within this assertive poetry of meaning. The language looks
outward with a simple, denotative potential—even "nothing" is
transformed into an active noun:

> But desire outstrips these hands that a nothing fills.

The language is referential, since it is ideally located within a
version of experience, and in that manner by which everything is
rendered 'concrete' and 'personal' by the tone of the poem. Everything is mediated through a single level of language that transforms even apparently subtle statements into a dense and simplistic
language of private experience:

> Brain in deft opacities
> Walled in translucencies, shuts out the world's knocking.

There is no variation of emphasis here, and no fullness of language;
there is only the central statement. The writing has a strained,

123

positivistic quality, and that heaviness of emphasis which is designed to make a point. We are engaged in a single perspective, among controlling forms, that has to be assumed to be the voice of the poet; its manner is concrete and ostensibly possessed of "truth". But what constitutes this truth?

It must be that of the self elucidating the world, since this is the central dispensation of the poetry. But the private self has by this time become a narrow and attenuated thing. The only way to give it substance is to transform the 'I' into an object, but Hughes can only do this through a kind of inverted humanism. There is a simple reversal of values, which is no less a humanism because the context of value has changed. Here, from *Ghost Crabs* is this new sense:

> They are the powers of this world.
> We are their bacteria
> Dying their lives and living their death.

It is the paradigmatic "we" to which subjectivity must cling, and through which it becomes an object. The theme of the "unconscious" and what has been called "its forces of evil" are partially symbolised in this poem, and it is a force that is continually evoked in the verse of Hughes. That entity which comes to its full potential in structuralist method is turned into a pseudo-mythic container of "meaning", and is used to carry on those conventional distinctions of "inner" and "outer" reality, truth and untruth. Humanism simply changes its terms in order to retain its values.

But the central weakness of the self, in clinging to a false objectivity, becomes apparent at the thematic level of Hughes's poetry. His themes are commonly those in which men are turned into objects by death or suffering, and a false subjectivity generates Hughes's attachment to brute or inanimate life. It is significant that a human world of "feeling" and moral experience is projected by Hughes onto the animal world. The hawk, snake, otter and thrush all either parody or imitate the truths of humanism:

> My eye has permitted no change
> I am going to keep things like this
> (from *Hawk Roosting*)

124

The Romantic 'I' can find a new home and

> The forever itself is a circling of the hooves of horses.

It is a paradoxical humanism that cannot discover Man's "values" within Man himself, and that must locate them elsewhere in order to keep them safe and render them visible. These values are located in *Crow*, for example, which is Hughes's narration of a bird that contains precisely those forces that were once discovered within the human world. It suggests that the human world is in decay, and so it must create the "unconscious" in order to create new values out of the old. As long as the poetry of Hughes retains its private voice, it repeats at a thematic level its own hollowness. Humanism is a spent force, which can only be invoked by a pure act of anthropocentrism, in which a bird can "stand for" man just as the language of Hughes's poetry can "stand for" a human truth:

> His prison is the earth. Clothed in his conviction
> Trying to remember his crimes.

This is the attenuated language of moral experience and subjective truth.

But subjectivity is not merely a rhetorical force, to be excised and quickly forgotten; the writings of Robbe-Grillet, for example, and the investigations of the phenomenologists redefine it outside a context of meaning and aesthetic value. Subjectivity in this sense resides in the gesture, in the manner of writing, and not in any value or human 'truth'. There is an Anglo-Saxon poetry which has inherited this novel sense of the self; it is a poetry that draws its major resources from a French tradition, and thus exists in the sharpest contrast to the "new poetry" of England although it became noticed at much the same time. It has been called the "New York school" but this is a geographical irrelevance, and there are two very different poets within the "school", Frank O'Hara and John Ashbery, who create a unique space for the experience of subjectivity.

The work of O'Hara might seem lyrical, since it uses a personal speech and not a formal language. But this speech does not have the voice of a subject which embodies 'truth' or emotion; it uses

a voice that is more relaxed than that, and less conscious of
itself:

> Totally abashed and smiling
>
> > > I walk in
> > > sit down and
> > > face the frigidaire
>
> > it's April
> > no May
> > it's May

This is very close to demotic speech; the poetry has an ease and
a directness that follow the rhythms of conversation and not, as
in the case of the English "new poetry", the structures of regular
form. There is an enlargement of line and a loosening of structure
within O'Hara's poetry that engages a new kind of poetic language;
to say that it is informal and discontinuous is one way of noting
that its voice has no fixed or central perspective. There is no 'I'
mastering its effects, since there is no experiential truth to be conveyed, but a steady attention to the procedure of the poem itself.
For the English poetry of Hughes, it is a question of discarding
the variation and strength of language in order to recreate significance or to describe the problems of the tiny self. In the poetry of
O'Hara, the vagaries and the unmediated life of speech deny the
formal completeness of a 'content':

> How funny you are today New York
> like Ginger Rogers in *Swingtime*
> and St. Bridget's steeple leaning a little to the left.

A conversational ease is not, of course, a new thing; it is present
in the public poetry of the first modernism in England, but it became more and more formalised until it developed into a pure
rhetoric of meaning. O'Hara discards these rhetorical forms and
returns to an imitation of speech that is no more now, than it
was at first, at the service of a 'private' voice. O'Hara's novel sense
of the personal will have to be defined here. For him, it is a way
of confirming the pure arbitrariness and fiction of his poetry, since
its voice resides on a perfect surface; there is a continual play of
irony that gives the language a vibrancy, distancing any meaning
or exemplary experience:

> I have been to lots of parties
> and acted perfectly disgraceful
> but I never actually collapsed
> oh Lana Turner we love you get up

Since there is nothing to be 'said', everything can be included; and since at the centre of the language is the active process of the poem itself, every external reference and object lies somewhere on the periphery. And this includes, most of all, the ubiquitous and apparent 'I'. It is not a subjective 'I' that discovers its values within the world, but one that can be as excessively general or as excessively particular as the events and signs mediated through the poetry. There is no personal 'expression', since the dichotomy of 'inner' and 'outer' reality—which is so pervasive in English poetry —is absolved by a continual regard for the surface of things:

> I have a hamburger and a malted and buy
> an ugly NEW WORLD WRITING to see what the poets
> in Ghana are doing nowadays
>   I go on to the bank
> and Miss Stillwagon (first name Linda I once heard)
> doesn't even look up my balance for once in her life

There is a new sense of being personal and expressive, in the interrogation and in the eventual affirmation of the gesture and activity of the surface of language.

The poetry of John Ashbery shares this concern for a language which, although assured and relaxed, manifestly "says" nothing. It is a literature, and Ashbery's poetry has a formal self-consciousness which recognises its special position. There is a largeness and an elaboration of language which create a beautiful surface, and counter the silence of the world. It is as if Ashbery's intuition, that literature can carry no "meaning" within itself, encourages a resonance and grace that seems most aesthetic when it is not so:

> Yet all would finish at the end, or go undreamed of
> It was a solid light in which a man and woman could kiss
> Yet dark and ambiguous as a cloakroom,
> No noise was to underline the notion of its being
> Thus the thing grew heavy with the mere curve of being
> As fruit ripens through the long summer before falling.

127

There is a strength and fullness of continuity within the writing here, and it is this continuity itself which dispels the illusion of 'content'. The almost random accumulation of images and the steady movement of the line afford only the pleasure of their own progress, since they are charged with an absence of meaning. The poetry is without expressive feeling in this sense, since it continually presents the language of feeling without enacting it. There is a commitment to 'meaning', but it is one that becomes self-reflective and makes a literature out of the attempt itself. Ashbery seems condemned to a perpetual invention of meaning within the poem, an attempt continually made and continually lost. The poem, however, stops just short of complete self-sufficiency, leaving the poet in the middle of an ambiguity that is fortunately a resourceful one:

And a feeling, again, of emptiness, but of richness in the way
The whole thing is organised, on what a miraculous scale

And it is not a simple truth that this scale can be both very large, since it is the scale of language, and yet very small:

So that a stamp could reduce all this
In detail, down to the last autumn leaf.

There is, then, an invention and re-invention of meaning with Ashbery's poetry—and the attempt creates a rhetoric that barely stands out on the surface of the poetry. But it does do so, and there are small conceits and figures that elicit the response but are continually undercut by ambivalence and doubt. In Joyce, the access of stylistic self-consciousness creates a wealth of texts and voices, but for Ashbery it has a more subtle and uniform presence. There is a continual redefinition in the manner in which the poem comments upon its own progress:

It is time now for a general understanding of
The meaning of all of this. The meaning of Helga, importance
of the setting etc.

and in the manner in which different kinds of language, placed within that same space of ostensible reference, counterpoint and

128

drain the meaning out of each other. Reflective generalisation, demotic cliché and personal lyricism revolve around each other in a continual movement of sense. There is no one perspective for all of this, since it is the dissolution of the classical spatiality—if I may put it that way—of English poetry. Even the 'I' is open to doubt and to sudden transformation:

> And I have an intuition that I am that other 'I' with
> which we began.

The ambiguity and irony that play over the surface of Ashbery's poetry derive from the differences which have been at the centre of this analysis of modernism. Ashbery creates a poetry out of the irresolution of rhetoric and literature, language and meaning, the possibilities of autonomy and the claims of private experience.

But Ashbery does not question the strategy of 'poetry' itself; for him it is still that area which constitutes truth even in his act of interrogating it. There is a sense in which he has formed an aesthetic from the conflict between self and language; the voice can be ironically effaced only to reappear as the completed design of the poetry. But there is a poetry which totally excises the realm of the voice and its experience, in a formal meditation upon the status of poetry itself. This is in part a result of the influence of structuralist method, which deconstructs what seems most permanent or most immediate, upon contemporary poetry. But there is another scholarship of modernism. It is that acquisition of an historical consciousness of style that has, in the work of Joyce and Eliot, become characteristic of our own cultural modernism; and there is one contemporary English poet, J. H. Prynne, who has gained access to these heightened possibilities of the language.

His is the first poetry to exercise the full potential of the written language. I could put the point another way by noting that his poetry excises completely the role of the poetic 'voice', whether as a personal or as a synthetic medium of expression, and so it moves beyond the range of purely aesthetic effects. His poetic forms offer a writing that calls into question our conventional response to what we think of as 'poetic' and what we think of as 'non-poetic'. Prynne's *Kitchen Poems*, for example, are described as "news-items" and they move away from any version of a poetic 'truth':

> The grid is another sign, is knowledge
> in appliqué-work actually strangled and latticed
> across the land, like the intangible consumer
> networks

The contemporary abstractions here, and the syntactical force which holds them within the same discursive context, exert an unfamiliar pressure upon the language. It has a self-certainty and a formal control that change the conventional experience of reading; we are not asked to participate in the lucidity and harmony of the poetry, we can only recognise its exterior signs. The question need not be—is this really poetry?—since we are presented with a new kind of language. It has a completely written surface:

> Here then is the purity of
> pragmatic function:
> we give the name of
> our selves to our needs.
> We want what we are.

This is perfect statement, constituted by a technical and historical writing that does not have the proportion or inflection of a poetic voice. It is not an affective language, but neither does it have any extrinsic reference. There is only a marginal denotative potential since the language aspires toward completeness and self-sufficiency. There is an absence of essentially poetic statement, since it is the formal and written attributes which give it its status. Prynne can retain varieties of contemporary language—financial, sociological, historical, lyrical, scientific—within a written paradigm which changes their function. Here is a 'lyric' which displays this new proficiency of the language:

> By such resounding
>   as by spherical
> harmonics is truth
>   in exact flux

130

come among men

        Quartz crystal

frequency standard

        madrigalian

brightness, bring

        the limits of parody

in the snowy cloud.

It is a literature appearing, since these variations of language and meaning have no reference to anything except the presence of their written form. The dispensation of poetry has now been changed, since it is now that area in which every kind of language can emerge into its historical and technical substance. If form becomes the arbiter of this language, we may expect elaboration and repetition as language unfolds into its own space, and it is within the interplay of these forms that we recover the quality of a language that exists somewhere between use and contemplation. But no literature emerges without causing tension and an irresolution. In Prynne, no less clearly than in Ashbery, ambiguity is caused by a language coming into itself against the power of that aesthetic context which had given it meaning and strength for so long. But Ashbery still retains an over-riding poetic voice to control this tension, while Prynne explores it upon the written surface of his literature.

Prynne's recognition of the absolute relativity of all forms of language, so that any one 'style' is an unnecessary intrusion upon the language, is one that is explored very differently in the work of certain contemporary French poets. The work of Denis Roche is to be considered here; he has been attached to the *Tel Quel* group, who have developed and extended structuralist method with that rhetorical and sometimes destructive certainty which is characteristic of French intellectual movements. But Roche's poetry, or what he calls his 'texts', does not have the self-certainty of pure theory. Within his writings, a literature appears but it is one with all the tension and impermanence that we have seen to be customary to it.

It has, first of all, certain features which firmly locate it within the orbit of modernism; we read a language that constitutes itself beyond an authorial 'I' and outside the aesthetic contexts of

131

'meaning' and 'experience'. The language seems arbitrary in a radical way:

> Sans audace, l'hyperbole, mon enjambement de
> Balcon en balcon vert, en droit ligne je me
> Prolonge comme le paysage vers une nouvelle
> fournée mortuaire, vers sa tombe de toute façon

Distinct areas of discourse are contingent upon one another, so that the complete effect is both one of the progress and disjunction of sense. It could be described as 'abstract' since it has no reference beyond its syntactical claims. Roche has talked of "a desire to negate or deny completely everything that could be said to belong to poetry and everything which could be said to separate poetry from all other literary genres or directions of research". There is no one language which can harbour a specially 'poetic' style, or a special type of 'poetic' meaning; there is only the language. We accede to the grace of its forms, but the language of Roche does not have the certainty of Prynne or the harmony of Ashbery. For Prynne, it is the actual dispensation of literature which is invested in those forms which are displayed like objects while, for Ashbery, it is his submerged aesthetic voice which is released by their activity. But in the poetry of Roche, the presence of form is keenly felt as a boundary; it has an all too tangible presence which, although it is the first experience of the new literature, is continually evaded by the language even in the process of its formation.

> 40 forme similaire a la précé-
> dente avec ailettes relevées en forme de gros volume.

The assertion of form becomes ironic here, and it is an irony which can be recognised in the hyphenated emphasis. The use of capitals at the beginning of each line is designed to stabilise these forms, but the use of run-on words emphasises not so much the unique reflexes of the speaking voice (as it might, for example, in the poetry of Gerard Manley Hopkins) but the mysterious chance of language which is not quite congruent with the experience of form. It is as if the form itself generates its own opposite since the form, the literature, takes on such prominence that it hardly seems able to support itself against the blankness of the page which surrounds it. It is that same ambivalence which invaded the language and topography of Mallarmé's poetry. Literature emerges as completely as it can in Roche's texts, but its autonomy and permanence are immediately cast into doubt.

Denis Roche suggests another aspect to the silence of meaning within literature. It is only by the willed activity of the reader that a significance can be drawn from his writing; the links between phrases and words are unstable, and there is an equivocation of meaning and image that exists above the surface of the poetry in perpetual anticipation of its own coherence. The act of reading— generally neglected in orthodox aesthetics—is here seen to be absolutely essential, and it may be that the poet's self-reading is the foundation of a literature. This seems paradoxical after my description of literature as the display of fiction within its own arbitrariness. But to say that the act of reading is the source of interpretation is not to make a simple humanistic or phenomenological point, since what is involved is not the access to another consciousness nor the attempt to recognise our own image within the writing. The act of reading has to be understood in a different context. If 'poetry' is no longer a separable quality of language, and if we are offered instead discourse simply in one of its formative texts, then we will read and deconstruct 'poetry' on terms that are methodologically constant and uniform. These terms are the "lexies" of structuralist analysis, or the measure of the ideal reader's attention. Denis Roche constructs each line and phrase within this idealised structure of reading, so that the particular life of his poetry lies in the combined presence of discursive and phonetic units, which exist in a continual state of tension with each other and with the reader who must reconstruct them and thus give the stamp of verity to the ostensible form of the literature. The multiform effect of the poetry seems to hover, to be perpetually present and yet nowhere stated.

The thematic and syntactical disjunctions which create this effect are, of course, reminiscent of surrealist poetry, but the language of Denis Roche is very different:

> Très gatés chez eux en fait de paysages de ce genre
> Mais du monde même de la naissance au génie occulte
> Capitaine guerrier noir. Ditto dieu de la guerre où. . . .

The progress of this poetry has nothing to do with any humanist vision of the 'unconscious' as a network of analogic correspondences: it has to do with the notion of permanent form. The concern is also, in a sense, to elicit "la matière première" of language, but at the first level at which it is perceived: the gestural phrase with its particular and unmediated life before the bondage of reference. We can still be convinced of this autonomy within the poetry of Roche, of its existence beyond a rhetoric of meaning, but we are offered a language more irresolute and therefore more complex than that within the poetry of Ashbery or Prynne. It is not now the tension which arises from 'meaning' usurping the original functions of language, but rather of the recognition that form must be completed by our own interpretation of it—although I myself, 'the reader', am the interpretation of a text which is no longer visible to me. This is the circle of modernism, and it is one which we can now explore.

The autonomy of form, and the return of language to its historical substance, practised first by Mallarmé and Nietzsche and formalised by De Saussure, is now an evident fact. It has become the prevailing direction of modernism, and it has now reclaimed other forms of expression—notably those of painting and music. I have represented language in one of its metaphors as aspiring toward the status of 'object', and it may be intriguing to notice the status of the object in that creative discipline where it is most apparent: that of painting. Again, the economic status of painting makes for an accelerated development which, although in no sense prognostic, has a certain relevance to the theme. I am thinking particularly here of "pop art", once fashionable and once even considered 'modern', which presents in a total, albeit naïve, fashion the most available qualities of modernism. The works of Andy Warhol and Roy Lichtenstein are in context here.

They are both fascinated by industrial techniques. It is both a thematic concern (the soup-can and the cola bottle are its objects) and a methodological one (silk-screen printing and mechanical reproduction become very important for the completed artefact). And their painting becomes 'object' in the most obvious way, flattened and reduced as it is by the industrial process. It becomes an industrial 'product', and so the ironic emblem of consumerised society; it certainly loses that unique 'presence' which had come to be associated with the 'work of art' formed by unique and individual 'genius'. The objectness of "pop art" is one that forms itself outside a ritualistic or iconic tradition; there is no longer a hierarchy of subject-matter, since the content of the art is the variety of style itself: "pop art" uses industrial imagery in the same spirit as it parodies the inherited artistic tradition. Warhol's thousand Mona Lisas could be cited here, as could Lichtenstein's 'expressionistic' brush strokes which repeat mechanically the once personal and uniquely evocative gestures of abstract expressionism. It is reminiscent of the Platonic description of art as the imitation of an imitation of reality, but what has now gone forever out of reach is the realm of human experience itself. When "pop art" represents itself as an object, it becomes an art-for-itself. It is an art that uses other art as its subject matter, and so displays the same stylistic and historical self-consciousness which appears in the literature of modernism. When art regards or parodies itself, the cultural tradition is destroyed as readily as it once was in the work of Marcel Duchamp. This denial of the aesthetic tradition can be put in another context by noting that the presence of perspective and illusion is heightened in "pop art": it renders a cultural tradition entirely transparent, and that habit of mind which seeks for realistic content and human significance is parodied and, once parodied, loses its force.

There has been a general identification of "pop art" with "pop culture", as though its industrial images were in some way symbolic or at least representative. But "pop art" does not have the same innocence of content, and it has indeed been one of the salient features of modernism that it has been indifferent to, and generally estranged from the popular culture. A Marxist interpretation might for once be plausible here, since to point to the growing 'objectness' and distance of art from any idea of 'man' is to come close to the vocabulary of alienation.

I have implied that popular culture is possessed of a radical innocence, and this is in fact its distinctive quality. It is within this very culture that a conventional humanist aesthetic re-appears within a context that stridently proclaims itself as 'modern' and 'new', and the culture is established upon an historical ignorance that is very different from the self-consciousness of modernism. It is only in the rock music of the 'counter-culture', for example, that we can recognise the naïve rhythms and harmonies of nineteenth-century European tonality. Similarly, the call for personal 'liberation' which became fashionable in the 'sixties is the refrain of a nineteenth-century ideology. Pop lyrics and 'beat poetry' revive a Victorian pastoralism with the icons of 'love' and 'freedom' from mechanised society. Theirs is a counter-culture only in the sense that it returns to an idealised humanism which the modern movement had overturned in Europe.

The central role of popular music and popular poetry in our time (and here I mean such established poets as Philip Larkin as well as the even better established lyrics of such as Rod Stewart) is to sustain certain responses which are most appealing because they are most familiar. But these responses rest upon a form of self-enjoyment, and turn into a humanistic kitsch. There is no distance between ourselves and those expressions which we promote as "vital" or "lyrical", since we simply sustain our own values in the act of reading or perceiving them. The popular film and the popular novel (Iris Murdoch as much as Harold Robbins) share these rhetorical features of popular culture, since they embody human figures mouthing typical or 'realistic' passions within an ordered speech, which has as its context a unified action proceeding from a beginning to a conclusion. They are the contours of a simplistic aesthetic. The television and the newspaper, also, remain innocent of their highly specialised form, and direct us to the 'real' world which is mediated through them. Theirs is a world of sensory stimulation in which content is seen as separate from form, persuading us of our experience and offering no release from it.

I do not want to oppose modernism to popular culture in order to draw facile distinctions. The world is a sphere of original and unpredictable play, and the return to a conventional view of human nature in certain forms of modern art ("earth art" and "happenings" were once in vogue) suggests a complexity of development which I can only remark on here. My theme has simply been that of modernism, and that, too, bears no easy development within itself. This has already become evident in the irresolution of such contemporary writings as those of Denis Roche, but it can also be seen elsewhere. The affirmation of the autonomy and arbitrariness of language took 'objectness' as one of its metaphors, but this generalisation runs into peculiar difficulties when we examine the development of the 'object' out of "pop art". For modernism seems most pervasive in 'minimal art', a movement which takes its initiative from earlier achievements in objectivity. It is a sculptural discipline, and three dimensional forms are created. The work has an absolute simplicity: primary forms (cubes, spheres, rhomboids and so on) are situated in their own space and, as Carl André puts it, "things exist in their elements, not in their relations". In minimal art, all parts of a sculpture are subordinated to a primary shape which is, simply, in existence. It displays no surface markings or organisational complexity which would allow a human reading of its presence. But it is this last quality, this 'presence' which is so forceful for those who have viewed minimal forms, which we must discuss. The quality of 'presence' has been previously aligned with a conventional aesthetic of individual or ritualistic expression. The works of "pop art" or the writings of Denis Roche have no presence, since it has been excised by a radical self-consciousness. But these simple forms of minimal art, apparently paradigmatic of the whole course of modernism, are charged with presence. They have attained an absolute objectness and arbitrariness, and yet they possess a dramatic and human quality. It is a strange inversion. Art has entered into an exact opposition with the spontaneity and relativity of human existence, and for that very reason it seems most human. These minimal art forms seem archetypal, and confront the human agent with an authentic 'essence'. They mimic what is the most enduring drama of life, that illusion which humanism had established as "permanence" and "unity". Modern art returns to the space of a rational aesthetic.

I can put it no better than that, since I am left with a paradox which cannot be transposed. The formal disciplines of sculpture and painting return to a restatement of an orthodox humanism, and with their drive toward simplicity and sublimity they recall the early formulae of Baumgarten and Burke, of Arnold and Coleridge. Even the 'object', which has been a continual analogy for

137

modernism during this analysis, disappears in the subsequent progress of artistic activity. "Conceptual art" abandons the material object altogether, and "earth art" returns to the human surface of the world. In this last sense, the theme of this book comes full circle. It is as if the phenomenology of Husserl, once a radical critique of orthodox consciousness, had entered the popular artistic mind, and had become the new humanism to which artist and audience alike can attach themselves. But if modernism is reversed in contemporary artistic activity, it has nothing like so simple a fate in relation to language and literature. Literature has always established within itself a certain ambivalence, and even in Roche and Prynne there is a contrast pulling toward reference and human significance. It may be that modernism bears most fruit when it resides in this tension, and it is in this context that we may expect something less dramatic but more resourceful than the operations of modern art: we are returning to the possibilities of language.

There is no more important reading here than the work of Jacques Lacan and of Jacques Derrida. They discuss the possibilities of language with more enthusiasm and more complexity than those who have turned linguistic or structuralist methods into a new positivism. Lacan, for example, locates the claims of language within an area that brings out their latent ambiguity, an ambiguity so foreign to the relentless progress of painting. Lacan situates language within the domain of psycho-analysis. The work of Freud has so far made only a brief appearance, since it was only during the 'fifties that his texts began to have a formative effect upon the European tradition. But now, toward the end of this analysis, Lacan's interpretation of Freudian theory becomes relevant since it comes to sustain the primacy of language. There is a fundamental analogy of language and the unconscious in structuralist enquiry, since they are both "form and not substance". It is this intangible but vital relation which Lacan elucidates in *Language and Self*: "For Freud, the dream has the structure of a sentence . . . the unconscious is not the primordial nor the instinctual, and elementarily it is acquainted only with the elements of the signifier." The popular conception of the unconscious as the repository of a hidden content of "needs" and "desires" is dis-

138

placed by an analysis which takes language as its model. The unconscious manifests the whole structure of language, both its arbitrariness and its difference. The description of literature can change its terms here, and it can be seen as having the same function as primal narcissism: it is an attempt to order the world within the autonomy and stability of complete self-identity. But this is too simple an identification. Lacan equates the unconscious with the signifier—a term which denotes the word, as the sign which exists without reference or 'meaning'. It is this dwelling within the signifier which is central to Freudian analysis, since "the putting into words of the event determines the lifting of the symptom". Lacan's therapeutic understanding is one that is established upon the substance of the language, since it is "the Word" that acts as an intermediary between the patient and the analyst, and it is the Word that confers 'meaning'. This is its power, and its permanent weakness. For it is within the domain of language that man seeks and finds his obsessions: "I identify myself in Language, but only by losing myself in it like an object." Language is not a transparent realm of easy access, but an opaque and arbitrary language which both offers and denies human meaning. And in Lacan's sense of "message" is that ambiguity which has been central to this analysis: "The unconscious is that discourse of the Other, where the subject receives, in the inverted form suited to the promise, his own forgotten Message."

What is this forgotten message, and what are these obsessive symptoms from which we seek recovery? They exist in the tension between word and language: "The symptom resolves itself entirely in a language analysis, because the symptom itself is structured like a Language, because it is from Language that the Word must be delivered." The Word is that hiatus in the autonomous structure of signifiers—a hiatus which can be named as the "signified", the "content" or the dream of 'meaning'. The signified, this image or concept beyond language, has been lost within the arbitrariness of language, but it is this vestigial referring power of language which has to be exorcised in analysis in order to allow the patient's free access into language, where he may be himself once more: "Man speaks out but it is because the symbol has made him Man." When the patient attempts to recover his own

139

Word, his own "meaning", in dream or in neurosis, he is always searching for the source of, or a point of entry into, the language; this is the lack which is felt in obsessive symptoms—that point at which "meaning" once entered into language, and which has now been lost. It could be said that the Word is that point of perfect symmetry at which a word is equivalent to a thing, a symmetry where an original life replete with meaning and significance might be recovered. I am reminded here of the paradisaical myth of that time when name and essence were one; the theological doctrine concerns their separation at the Fall of Man, so that the essence of the world can now only be recovered by a perpetual and inconclusive exegesis. That mythic time of ostensible and immediate meaning is the paradise to which hysterics continually return, and it is one which haunts us during this age when language speaks us.

I have put rhetorically here what has been the main statement of this analysis. Within Lacan's interpretation of Freudian texts there exists that tension which constituted the life of Baudelaire and the labour of Mallarmé. It is that pressure within language to a knot of meaning, an access to the world beyond the claims of the signifiers which name it. Mallarmé had first introduced the ambivalence of presence and absence into his poetry, and it was the concept of absence which De Saussure had formalised in his concept of the pure differentiality of language. But it is Freud who further elaborates upon this insight in his description of child's play. The child shouts "ah" at the presence of an object, according to Freud, and "oo" when he throws it out of sight. Here is Lacan's interpretation: "The child in question would associate the appearance and disappearance of the toy which he alternatively threw away and drew back again with the vowel sounds 'o' and 'a'. which Freud interpreted as those of the German words for "gone" (Fort!) and 'here' (Da!)." One sound conjures up, and makes apparent, the absence of that which has been lost from view. The fullness of the sound mediates the loss of the object, since it exists on the same terms as its phonetic opposition, "a". Does not absence itself emerge here as the proper role of the word?

It is at this point that the work of the French philosopher, Jacques Derrida, comes into focus. Derrida's theme is one which

THE PURSUIT OF MODERNISM

has been central to this analysis since he moves from a Lacanian analysis of personal speech to the more opaque and ostensibly more familiar area of the written language. This is not a casual transition, and it may be one that changes the face of knowledge. According to Derrida, the preference for speech over writing, which is solely a European phenomenon, is one that has disavowed the world of signs in favour of that presence and that content which the spoken word claims by virtue of its origin in the human voice and in gesture. It is, essentially, an appeal to a signified (le signifié) against the signifier (le signifiant). The signified is the body of the human message, and its image is one that has larger consequences: the realm of 'being' is its horizon, since this is the largest 'meaning' of all—"L'être est le signifié transcendental".

This faith in the human and living significance of speech is one that determines a special kind of truth, or rather 'truth' itself. In the writings of Aristotle, the voice was that which is closest to soul and to sense. And the word has always been known as "l' unité élémentaire et indécomposable du signifié et de la voix, du concept et d'une substance d'expression transparente". It is a necessary corollary of this that "Le logocentrisme serait donc solidaire de la determination de l'être de l'étant comme présence". It is this ideology of presence which appears within rationalism and the first modernism, an ideology in which truth resides in the positive sign, in the word; it is this concept of the word that illustrates the theological spirit of our cultural inheritance: "Le signatum renvoyait toujours comme à son referent, à une res, à un étant crée ou en tout cas d'abord pensé et dit, pensable et dicible au présent éternel dans le logos divin et précisément dans son souffle."

I have quoted at length here from Derrida's *De La Grammatologie*, in order to elucidate that historical nexus which has formed all previous concepts of language. It is the metaphysic of "truth" and "presence" which defined the order of written language as somehow secondary and derivative. It has conventionally been seen as the transcription of the spoken word and its human presence, and so as a set of mute signs to be organised and tabulated. Writing was viewed as an inferior operation because it does not

141

possess that absolute presence-to-itself, which has always been the rationalist criterion of subjectivity and its truth. But the movement of modernism has been one that has reclaimed the primacy and absoluteness of written discourse—it was that discourse which emerged as the substance of literature, and which was later formalised in linguistics. And it is this progress which Derrida evokes, in his description of the transition from "une époque historico-métaphysique" in which speech determines "la totalité de son horizon problematique", to our time in which language is "la guise ou le deguisement d'une écriture première". Writing is now that form which "determine le concept de 'signe' et toute sa logique", since it is "la condition de l'épisteme". Writing is no longer an image or a record of speech, but an alien form which harbours a significance very different from that of logocentrism and rationalism. It has excised the last vestiges of meaning, since its form is now that of "la signifiant de la signifiant". The desire for meaning within language is precisely that quest for a lost object—in a word, death. But how are we to describe this discrete world of signs?

Its significance is an alien one, and perhaps impossible to grasp: "L'écriture est cet oubli de soi, cette éxteriorisation . . ." since writing is conceived as pure absoluteness and exteriority. It is non-phonetic, and it forms an arbitrary "trace". This notion of "trace" is central to Derrida's whole argument since "la trace est en effet l'origine absolue du sens en général". It is not a positive or material force, but a sense conceived in opposition and paradox: ". . . la trace est l'ouverture de la première extériorité en général, l'énigmatique rapport du vivant à son autre . . . la non-présence de l'autre inscrite dans le sens du présent, le rapport à la mort comme structure concrète du présent vivant." It is that original Other, which has been defined through this analysis as nothingness and absence. The trace is, in fact, the original absence since "la disparition de la vérité comme présence" is the condition of the writing which constitutes it. The written trace is an effect without a cause for "la trace est immotivée, il faut penser la trace avant l'étant."

Now, beyond the categories of presence and being, a familiar theme emerges. Writing, for Derrida, is the epiphany of differ-

THE PURSUIT OF MODERNISM

ence as in the "ŏ" of the child's phonetic play. It is that assertion of difference which must occur in any utterance: even the
world of messages is "originairement et essentiellement trace".
Writing constitutes an original, irreducible difference. There is no
spoken language which stays untouched by writing, and we must
assume an "archi-écriture" as the foundation of all expression—
an original trace which manifests itself in that human or linguistic
play beyond truth and meaning.

And it is within this context that the particular strategy of literature can be understood. In the pure absence of meanings, language
can return to a state of play (or of difference) and literature becomes "le jeu de la forme" since it is "ce jeu, pensé comme
l'absence du signifié transcendental." But the primacy of the
written language creates another and a more specialised discipline
—it might be described as the science of signs and which Derrida
calls "grammatologie", or the science of language from which all
extrinsic relations have been banished. Grammatologie covers every
expression that is estranged from the voice and its realm of presence: the cinema, sculpture and even "d'écriture militaire ou poli-
tique". Writing bears within itself the necessity of its own
critique; its task is to demystify itself of any signifying force, and
of any attempt to discover an existential foundation for itself.
Grammatologie is in this sense a necessary but unaccomplishable
discipline, since writing can never occupy that position of absolute
facticity. Derrida's texts, then, create a necessary myth; language
is perpetually distant from its origin, its irreclaimable being-in-
the-world, and is thus consigned to interpreting itself. The signs
of language refer only to other signs, and texts only to other texts.
Derrida's sense of écriture is one that encourages this sense of an
absolute form without origins, and it does so by asserting the
primacy of difference.

Lacan has a complementary insight into the analytical process:
". . . no meaning is sustained by anything other than reference
to another meaning." And the model of written language is not a
purely formal or specialised one, but one that encompasses our
largest concerns in this analysis: "La grammatologie ne doit pas
être une des sciences humaines, parce qu'elle pose d'abord, comme
sa question propre, la question du nom d'homme." The name, man,

is the name of that being who has throughout its existence dreamt of a full presence, of an origin and of an end. But our interrogation of language reflects back now upon a possible interpretation of man. Language manifests itself when it ceases to identify with "truth" or "meaning", and it may be that man will fully recognise himself when he ceases to search for an origin or a goal. It would be to pass beyond humanism, which seeks its foundation in the essence of *homo humanus*. This analysis has gone beyond aesthetics, and beyond the idea of subjectivity; it has perhaps also gone beyond the name of man.

Conclusions

I am not sure but I agree in Lamartine's prophecy that 100 years hence the Continent will be a great united Federal Republic and England, all her colonies gone, in a dull and steady decay.

Matthew Arnold, 1848

It is perhaps best at this point to provide some form of general statement, since this analysis has covered many and various activities. Modernism is that movement in which created form began to interrogate itself, and to move toward an impossible union with itself in self-identity. This is the life which first appeared in the writings of Mallarmé and Nietszche, and it finds its specific reference in the novel idea of literature. Language is seen to constitute meaning only within itself, and to excise the external references of subjectivity and its corollary, Man. Language thus moves beyond the instrumental language of positivism at the same time as it denies the force of humanism, and it is significant that the methods of positivism are now being used to salvage the name of Man under the guise of the social sciences.

This new autonomy and formal absoluteness of language has become the model which has been operating in art, in the development of linguistics, in structuralist method and in psychoanalytical therapy. It is the controlling image of our time, but one that has gone unrecognised in our own culture which has remained in the shadow of the first modernism of the seventeenth century. This was a modernism which initiated "experience" and "human nature" as moral categories, and it is within their significance that we still dwell.

But the development of a rational aesthetic can be most easily measured in the European texts. It appears as an idea of individual sensory gratification, subordinate to the uses of the reason, and

145

it is reversed by Marcel Duchamp's denial of formal lucidity and human use in the experience and creation of 'art'. Art comes to reside in its own formal investigation, and comes to retrieve its history. But what has persisted in England is the conventional aesthetic, which rests upon certain key notions of "subjectivity" and "experience", notions that were never properly analysed. In fact, it is only in certain European texts that the idea of subjectivity is questioned and revised. In the phenomenological writings of Husserl and Merleau-Ponty, there emerges a novel selfhood which has been disinherited from any rationalist or literary method. Perhaps this is a necessary extension of the withdrawal of language from the human world, since the redefined selfhood is one that exists prior to language and its relations, and is incarnate in the world. It is no longer dependent upon a metaphysic of presence and 'being', which is the foundation of humanism. Our national culture has played no part in this revaluation, and retains the idea of 'subjective' expression within the canons of literary realism. But the movement of modernism is not an easy nor an inevitable one; with the disintegration of the familiar rational and humanistic aesthetic, there has simply been an escalation of styles which promise perhaps only a new hermeneutics and not a permanent awakening.

It is clear that, now, England is a dispirited nation. The social weakness runs very deep, and does not yet seem close to any definition let alone resolution. This analysis has, I hope, marked out certain features of this decline. I have attempted to describe the impoverishment of our national culture and I hope to have demonstrated that, from the beginning of this century, it has rested upon a false base. The 'humanism' which the universities sustain, and which our realistic literature embodies, is the product of historical blindness. It has been associated with a sense of the 'individual' and of the 'community' which stays without definition, except in the work of some literary academics who appeal to a literary 'tradition'. But the actual facticity and autonomy of literature has not been recognised in this country, and so literary studies have been readily attached to such external pursuits as sociology and anthropology.

The context of this failure of our cultural and intellectual tradition has been the implicit refusal to operate upon anything other than an empirical and pragmatic base. There has been none of that formal self-criticism and theoretical debate which sustained European modernism: from those theoretical beginnings in France, in the avowal of "nothing" and "absence" against the positive dispensation of classical rationalism, it has been the creative discovery of theory which has enriched the quality of French culture. As our own universities split their concerns into more and more specialities, the paucity of their theoretical life becomes more and more evident in the apparently endless spirals of empirical enquiry. The humanism which we take to be our inheritance and our foundation—apparently unaware of its origin in the late seventeenth century—has turned out to be an empty strategy, without philosophical content or definitive form.

It is a paucity that, with certain few honourable exceptions, manifests itself in English creative writing. Our own literature has revealed no formal sense of itself and continues no substantial language. Our writing has acquiesced in that orthodoxy which has already been described, resting as it does upon a false aesthetic of subjectivity and a false context of realism. And it is this conventional aesthetic which has been reified into the English 'tradition'. The public for this literature is similar in most respects to the recipients of popular culture, and the writing of our time—specifically that which is constantly being described as "new"—confirms a similar set of values. Since there is no properly responsive public, there are only literary groups dominated by the popular media and by the fashionable concerns of the metropolis. England has insulated itself from the development of modernism.

How is this modernism to be best expressed? Perhaps it can be described as a sense of freedom. We no longer invest created forms with our own significance and, in parallel, we no longer seek to interpret our own lives in the factitious terms of art. Artistic forms are no longer to be conceived of as paradigmatic or mimetic. Our lives return to their own space, outside interpretation and extrinsic to any concern for significance or end. I might put this differently by suggesting that it is the ability of literature to explore the problems and ambiguities of a formal absoluteness which we will never experience. For these forms seem to proclaim the death of Man.

147

Index